TESTIMONIES
of a GOOD
GOD

BYRON VAN DER MERWE

Copyright Page

Testimonies of a Good God
Copyright© 2016 Byron van der Merwe
Living in Victory Ministries
ISBN 978-0-9956242-1-4

For more information about this book or to invite Byron to come and speak to your group, please go to

WWW.LIVINGINVICTORYMINISTRIES.COM

Contents

Dedication

I dedicate this book to my beautiful wife Tammie, our daughter Hannah, our son Joshua, my parents, and my brother Grant and sister-in-law Kerry. Thank you all for always standing with me and for all the support. I love all of you deeply. I would also like to thank Tammie's family for loving me and for making me a part of their family.

I also dedicate this book to Thomas Crickett. My friend, you were an inspiration and a great man of God. You may not be here on Earth anymore but we will meet again in eternity. I want this book to be a testimony of God's goodness to your family, even if it's just in a small way. So 25% of the after tax profits of this book will go to helping support your family. Love you Thomas.

Acknowledgements

I would like to thank Lisa Oliver for all of her hard work and support. Lisa, thank you for your encouragement.

Thank you to Patrick McCarthy for all the help, friendship and advice with the website and making it happen. Your contribution has been invaluable.

Thank you to Keath, Michelle and the team at Kingsgate Church for being who you are and doing what God has called you to do. As a team and a church, you all are truly an inspiration and a model of what the Kingdom of God should look like in everyday life.

Thank you to Brian Kettles for always encouraging me and for believing that God has great things in store.

Thanks to Rob and Natalie Pick for all of your hard work and help with this book.

Thank you to Sue Griggs for your input and encouragement on this project. I'm so very grateful.

Thank you Christy Lawrence for all the work you put in. You and Justin are truly a blessing to us.

Thank you Aksinia Tweeddale for your help, hard work and encouragement. I really appreciate you and Pasquale.

Thanks to everyone else who has already read this book and encouraged me to take a step of faith and publish it.

Endorsements

I have known Byron and Tammie for a few years now. I have had the pleasure of praying with them and have seen the authority and power of their prayers. Having just read this book I can see why they pray and speak the way they do. Byron is able to encourage and strengthen those who are in trouble or facing difficulties. You don't become an overcomer without going through some battles, so as you read about Tammie and Byron's journey you will be energised for your own breakthroughs and victories. Our Heavenly Father is indeed a Good God!

John Alcock
Co-founder of Mobilise Now ministries,
United Kingdom

I have known Byron & Tammie for about 8 years now. The two things that stand out above all else about them are they are humble people and they have incredible faith, especially in the area of finance.

They live by a simple paradigm that if it

says it in God's word then it must be true and I can base my life on it.

I know that at numerous times over these years, when faced with major financial decisions, I seek out their advice because I know it will be both faith filled and real.

I've also watched how Father has refined them over time and how they possess the humility to let him change them and make them more like Jesus.

You can trust the man writing these stories because they aren't pet theories or vain imaginations, they are the realities he and Tammie have faced together with Jesus.

Paul Harper
Pastor and Elder Kingsgate Church
Kingston upon Thames, United Kingdom

Congratulations Byron & Tammie, Your book is so full of wonderful testimonies of God's goodness upon your lives. It is a must read for every Christian whether they are or not facing giants, trials or tribulations. This book is jam packed with so many encouraging testimonies, all praise and glory to God – our good God who loves giving His children good gifts. Amen!!

May your sell thousands of copies of your book.

Blessings with our love.

Arnold & Gisela Nel
Lead pastors Lusaka Family Church,
Zambia

We have been friends with Byron and Tammie for many years now and have witnessed first-hand how they have stepped out in faith and in turn seen Gods faithfulness to them through their obedience to His call.

They are genuinely passionate about Jesus and have inspired us in so many ways to live a more obedient and generous life.

"Testimonies of a good God" will inspire you and fill you with Faith and Courage to step out and be obedient to Gods call on your life. – An excellent read!

Tim and Paula Petersen
Lead pastors CityHill Church Amanzimtoti,
South Africa

Introduction

This book is the result of a 16-year pursuit of God. It is the story of my life so far. My walk with Jesus and how He has come through for me in seemingly impossible situations. Having lost my sister, experiencing heartbreak after a failed relationship, nearly losing my brother and facing many other trials, I pray that you will find this story encouraging and faith building.

My prayer is that through the testimonies you read, you would not see me but see God, and see God for who He really is. He is a good God. He loves you, He will deliver you, He will cover you and He will protect you.

My desire is that through this book you will truly understand that with God nothing is impossible (see Matthew 19:26). I've seen first-hand that this is true, even when life hasn't always gone the way I wanted. Looking back over my life, the hand of God is so prevalent. He has remained so very close to me even when I wasn't aware of it.

Even during times when I was bitterly disappointed and life didn't seem fair - HE brought me through, and I have come out stronger and more convinced that God loves me unconditionally and that He is a good God.

I would encourage you to take this book as a testimony of what Jesus has done for me and begin to prophesy the same victory over your life (see Revelation 19:10b). If God did it for me, He can do it for you. Not that God is a formula. The way He has worked in my life may not be the way He will bring about victory in yours. Even the teaching chapters (Chapters 9 & 10) at the back of the book are tools, not rules. These are things God has shown me to keep me walking in His freedom. Ask Him to show you what will work for you.

I wish there was a simple answer to overcoming all of life's struggles. I haven't found there to be a quick "microwave answer" so to speak, but I do know the One who knows all the answers and has the solution to all of life's difficulties. His name is Jesus and the more I've gotten to know Him, the more grace and wisdom I've received to walk through life victoriously in every situation.

The Bible is not only the word of God but IS God (see John 1:1-5) and the Holy Spirit makes it come alive. Just learning or memorising the Bible without the Holy Spirit, in my experience, has been very unfruitful. However, I can honestly say that the greatest victories my wife Tammie and I have seen, have been in those moments where the Holy Spirit has highlighted scripture to us. We have meditated on those scriptures, taken communion over them and stood in agreement that God would honour His word. We took those words as our own and stood on the word of God (the Bible) until we saw breakthrough.

Some breakthroughs were instant but some have taken a few years to see complete healing or victory. Even now, as I release this book I am facing the biggest health challenge I have ever faced, but God is the same yesterday today and forever (see Hebrews 13:8). What God has done for us in the past, He can still do for us in the future. I have no reason to believe that the same God who brought me through into victory then will not continue to bring me through into victory now.

Truthfully, there have been times when believing God and trusting His word were hard. Especially when the situation seemed so opposite to what we know the Bible says. But the more I walk with the Lord, the more intimately I know Him. And the more I know Him and His word, the easier it becomes to walk in victory every day.

Tammie and I are just normal, everyday people. We don't speak Greek or Hebrew. We are two Christians who are relentless pursuers of His word and His presence. In a way I suppose we just have simple faith - what we read in scripture we have chosen to believe. The more we have believed the word of God, the more we have been able to navigate through life's challenges.

I pray that through this book God will give you a greater desire and passion for His word and that He will show you that He is still the God of miracles.

He wants to call you into a deeper and more intimate relationship with Him. The closer you get to Him, the more clearly you will hear Him. In Him is the solution to every problem you will ever face. Like I said, God is not a formula; He wants a relationship with you. His victory is not hidden from you, it's hidden for you. God already has a blessed plan for you.

I encourage you to stop limiting God whilst asking Him to bless your plans. Find out what His plan for you already is and jump into it because it's already blessed.

We are victorious and Jesus paid the full price for freedom. Now let's take hold of it by faith and move into more of the freedom that Jesus has already given us (see Galatians 5:1).

Hearing God

In this book I speak quite a lot about hearing God. I'm not talking about hearing an audible voice or anything like that, although that may happen for some people. I'm talking about the everyday relationship with God that is available to every Christian that has made Jesus their Lord.

The Bible is filled with accounts of people hearing and speaking to God. God spoke with Adam and Eve. He spoke to Moses face to face like a friend. God spoke to Joshua, to Samuel, to Nathan, to Solomon, to Elijah, to Saul who became Paul, to Ananias, to Stephen, to Simeon and many more, Old Testament and New Testament. (See notes below for scripture references).

In the New Testament, Jesus promises all of us the Holy Spirit, who will show us all things and remind us of everything Jesus has said to us (see John 14:26). If God speaks, and the Holy Spirit is God living in us and having a relationship with us, (see Romans 8:11), then it makes perfect sense that we can hear from Him and talk with

Him. God is alive. People that are alive, speak. Dead people don't speak. To have the Holy Spirit in us yet never having him speak to us is strange to me and is not congruent with God's word. If we believe He is alive then we must believe that He speaks.

Jesus also tells us in John 10:27 that His sheep know His voice and will follow Him. Psalm 23:1 describes the Lord as being our Shepherd - to lead, guide and protect us.

As the children of God, we are His sheep and He is our Shepherd. In the same way that sheep know and trust their shepherd when he calls them, we should be able to recognise God's voice when He speaks and then we should follow Him.

Notes: Genesis 2:15-20, Exodus 33:11, Joshua 1:1-3, 1 Samuel 3:4, 2 Samuel 7:4, 1 Kings 3:5, 1 Kings 17:8, Acts 9:4, Acts 9:10, Acts 6:10, Luke 2:26

1

Destruction or a Defining Moment?

I was born in South Africa to amazing parents. I was the middle child, having an older brother and a younger sister. Growing up we went to church, but for me at least there was no relationship with God. Most Sundays I would pretend to sleep in as long as possible so that I did not have to go to Sunday school. One of the few memories I have of church back then is that the pastor spoke about hearing God talk to him. At the time, I remember thinking, "God doesn't still talk to people."

Our lives as young children were fairly normal I suppose. We were a middle-class family with only my Dad working, and at times, there was "more month than money." Our home environment was good, nonetheless, and both my parents loved us very much. Life however, was about to change.

When I was twelve my sister Lynda began to suffer from very frequent migraines and headaches. She was eight years old at the time and after a few doctor appointments, as well as couple of weeks of constant headaches, they decided to investigate further.

About a week later, my parents said we were going away for the weekend to the beach. That Saturday morning, my mother and sister stayed at the accommodation, and my Dad, brother and I went down to the beach.

My Dad sat us down and said he needed to tell us something. He said the doctors had done various tests and discovered that my sister had a brain tumour. It was really big, and the doctors needed to operate as soon as possible. They had scheduled her for an operation the next week. The operation would take six or seven hours and she had roughly a 30% chance of survival.

How are you supposed to respond to news like that? At the time, all I could think about was how selfish I had been with my sister, how I always made her sit in the middle seat of the car and that now she may be dying. It's funny what goes through your mind when you are in shock. My brother and I both said we understood, but who at any age can really comprehend that kind of news?

The next week we were introduced to her doctor, and he said that he would do his best.

My sister was very calm. She had believed in Jesus since she was a little child; she would never let my Mom or Dad put her to sleep unless they first prayed with her and asked Jesus to look after her.

As I recall, she went in for the operation on a Saturday. To be honest, I don't remember a lot of the day, I only remember wondering if she would die and then my parents telling us that she had pulled through. The doctors had removed as much of the tumour as possible but were concerned that if they removed all of it she would be left with permanent brain damage.

She spent a long time in the hospital and when she was released, she and my Mom moved into accommodations at the hospital in Durban, where she was receiving radiation. My Dad, brother and I stayed in Pietermaritzburg, about 60 miles from Durban, where he worked and where we went to school. But we spent the weekends with my Mom and sister in the flat in Durban.

The radiotherapy had many side effects which left my sister feeling extremely unwell. It also affected her walking and due to the cortisone treatments it caused her to retain a lot of water and she got really big. This period of time was very difficult for Lynda and my parents. Unfortunately, people can be very insensitive. Lynda was often stared at because she was large and had lost her hair due to treatment.

Despite this the radiation seemed to work, and for the next year or so things seemed to be fairly smooth. However, my sister then started experiencing a lot of complications and ended up in the hospital for many weeks. During this time she had another operation to insert shunts that would release the pressure on her brain.

After she was released, she went back home and life carried on as normal for a few months, or as normal as it could be in that situation.

Looking back now, it must have taken an immense toll on my parents, but my brother and I never really saw it, as they both always put on a brave face for us.

Around two years after finding out she had cancer, Lynda began sleeping more and more. Then one day she began to have seizures. An ambulance was called and she was rushed to hospital. At the time her doctor was away on holiday, and the only other neurosurgeon in Pietermaritzburg was covering his patients. The new doctor did some tests and spoke to my parents and asked them what her doctor had told them. They said her doctor told them, considering what she had been through, she was doing okay.

The new doctor looked at my parents and said he was very sorry, but the brain tumour had grown substantially. There was nothing he could do. She was dying and would not leave the hospital alive. He didn't know how long she had, but he was certain she would die.

Nothing can prepare you for that. I suppose you just go numb. You never really think about death, or at least I didn't at the time. It can just sneak up on you.

We spent the next two days by her side 24-7 and some of our family members from around the country started to come to say goodbye. Through all of this, I don't remember my sister Lynda ever being angry, cursing God or losing faith in Him. If anything, I remember her still praying and asking Jesus to look after and protect her, as well as us.

On the second day, my brother and I had just returned home to get some rest. My Dad arrived shortly afterwards crying. He told us my sister had just passed away in my mother's arms.

We all hugged in disbelief. He then took us to the hospital so we could see Lynda and say goodbye. We lived literally across the road from the hospital, and 10 minutes later we were in her room.

I remember walking into the room and seeing my Mom still holding her. Lynda's body was there, but she had left. My Mom put her down, and we all sat in the room and cried. I remember a nurse came in to prepare the body to take to the mortuary. My Mom was furious and told her we hadn't even said goodbye yet.

The next few days were a bit of a blur, and about a week later we had the funeral. At that time, I didn't believe in Jesus or that a good God could ever let something like this happen. We had even taken Lynda to a healing meeting at a church, and they had anointed her with oil, prayed for her, and she still died. I was angry towards God.

At Lynda's funeral there were so many people that there wasn't enough room in the church. The only thing I remember clearly of that day was that we sang the hymn "The Lord is my Shepherd." To this day when I hear this song, I think of Lynda.

The next few months and years were very difficult on our whole family, especially on my parents. I think we were all disillusioned with life and didn't really know what to do or where to turn. My parents decided they could not live in Pietermaritzburg anymore as it brought back too many memories of Lynda. They decided we would move to Hillcrest, just outside Durban.

Losing their daughter was very difficult for my parents and only now being a parent myself can I begin to imagine what it must have been like for them. In the next few years that followed, we all just moved on, or tried to.

I really enjoyed school, excelled in swimming and spent most of my spare time in swimming training. I remember having a few Christian friends at school, but to be honest they really irritated me because I did not believe in this God they were telling me about. After all, why did He kill my sister and destroy my family?

My first year out of school, I worked for a transport company based in Durban. My role was to drive down to the port and make sure the company's trucks had the right documentation and were loaded correctly so they could be released from the port.

A few months into the job, I was driving in the car, and my vision disappeared. I couldn't see. I felt extremely dizzy and my vision began to blur in and out. I managed to pull over on the side of the road. By this time, I was getting really scared, and I thought perhaps I had been drugged. I had one of those original mobile phones that had a speed dial on it. I called the office and told them what was happening. They weren't sure what to do, but they called my brother and got him to come and pick me up.

My brother came and took me straight to the doctor. He examined me and said I needed to go to the hospital for observation. At the hospital they did some tests. At this stage I could now see again, but was still very dizzy.

The tests came back and showed nothing wrong. The doctors said I needed to go for a CAT (CT) scan to see what was going on in my brain. Fear gripped me. I was nineteen years old, and I wasn't ready to die. Did I also have a brain tumour like my sister?

They took me up to have the CAT scan and when I got there, one of the Christian girls I went to school with was working there, and she said she would pray that God would protect me.

The scan came back clear. I had never been so relieved in all my life! I was released from hospital a day or two later but still with constant dizziness.

The doctor said that there obviously was something wrong, but I would have to wait it out. That didn't help my nerves, because I thought at that moment I was going to die of some unknown disease. A few days later I went back to my General Practitioner (GP), and he said he would check my ears again. The hospital staff had done this a few times already and said my ears were fine. The GP looked in my ears and said he would like to flush my ears out as they looked dirty. While he was flushing my right ear, all of a sudden I heard a pop and something dropped out of my ear. Instantly the dizziness stopped, and I felt normal again. The doctor then discovered that the thing that had popped out was a piece of a silicone earplug I had used for swimming training. It had obviously broken off and lodged itself onto my ear drum.

That evening I received a call from a friend's mother, who always told me about Jesus. She said to me, "Byron, how's your ear doing?"

"What do you mean?" I asked. I had not told anyone about what had happened at the doctor's office. She said, "I have been praying and God told me that there was something stuck in your ear and when it comes out you will be fine." Wow, she really got my attention! How could she know this? Had God really spoken to her?

I began to get interested in this Jesus and decided to put my feelings about my sister aside for a while and go and see if there was anything to this "God thing." I called a Christian friend, Dom, and asked if I could go to church with him. I still remember asking what I should wear. He said, "Byron, our church is very relaxed. You can just wear underwear if you like." I was pretty nervous to say the least, and wondered if he was actually joking about the underwear.

When we arrived at church, it was weird and not what I thought it would be at all. Everyone seemed like they were really happy. "This is obviously one of those happy-clappy churches," I thought. "That's not for me."

But there was a strange peace there, and I was uncomfortably comfortable. I went back a few times and finally surrendered my life to Jesus after an altar call.

A new peace and joy began to flood my life. God had begun to reveal Himself to me, and I had an encounter with the Living God. God was no longer this guy who was mad at us and who sat in Heaven; He was this guy who was with me, right where I was, broken and all. God slowly began to restore me and more and more, I began walking in wholeness.

I have asked God many times about what happened with Lynda. I believe He has spoken to me and given me peace that it wasn't His perfect plan, but there are some things in life we are just not going to understand. I have all eternity with Lynda and plenty of time to chat with her and God about what happened. My role here on earth is to move on and allow God to remove all the hurt and live victoriously as a victor and not a victim.

No one in life has it easy and it's easy to think that we are the only person to go through hardships and that no one else understands. The truth is everyone has issues and troubles. We need to see the light at the end of the tunnel and see that some things will be left for eternity.

I encourage you if you have been through a loss, to look to Jesus and decide to let Him be Lord. Instead of spending your whole life asking why, make a decision to walk forward in victory and leave some chatting to Jesus for eternity. You can move forward whole and complete in Him.

I can honestly say that God has removed the hurt and sorrow in me from my sister passing away. I will never forget her, nor will I forget what happened, but I will not allow it to define the rest of my life. God is good all the time, even when I don't understand. I suppose for me, I've realised that everyone dies, and it's eternity that is important. Philippians 4:7 NIV says "The peace of God which transcends all understanding will guard your hearts and minds in Christ Jesus." There is peace available in the midst of not understanding.

It won't be all that long and I will be reunited with Lynda again. So I look forward to that day, but until then, I want to live every day full of hope, full of joy, knowing the future is bright because Jesus has my future. He has my life, it's in His hands, and He knew me before I was formed in my mother's womb (see Psalm 139:13). He knows how to restore me.

It's so interesting that we sang the hymn "The Lord is my Shepherd" at Lynda's funeral as it's from Psalm 23 (NIV), which reads:

> The Lord is my shepherd, I lack nothing.
> He makes me lie down in green pastures,
> he leads me beside quiet waters,
> he refreshes my soul.
> He guides me along the right paths
> for his name's sake.
> Even though I walk
> through the valley of the shadow of death,
> I will fear no evil,
> for you are with me;
> your rod and your staff,
> they comfort me.
> You prepare a table before me
> in the presence of my enemies.
> You anoint my head with oil;

my cup overflows.
Surely your goodness and love will follow me
all the days of my life,
and I will dwell in the house of the Lord
forever.

I have walked through the valley of the shadow of death. God has restored my soul and He has given me a place of peace. I am seated at His table, and my life is full. I am a blessed man! I have a wonderful family - all of whom now believe in God, a beautiful wife, a beautiful little daughter and a new born son. God is so good; He has restored my life. If He has done it for me, He can do it for you.

I encourage you to let Jesus in to your whole life, even into those places you don't want Him, those places in your life that have caused you to walk through the valley of the shadow of death. Stop camping in the valley. Come out instead, and sit at the table God has prepared for you. It's a good table, a feast set up just for you in the presence of your enemies. Don't allow hurt and fear to hold you back anymore. Jesus wants to give you rest and peace and joy that overflows. You can dwell in His house for evermore.

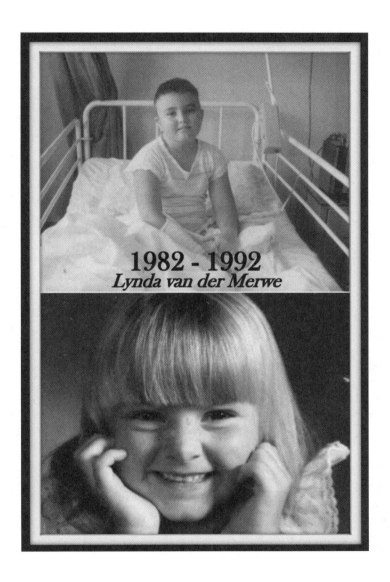

1982 - 1992
Lynda van der Merwe

TESTIMONIES *of a* GOOD GOD

2

The Tammie Factor

Like any guy, I have always found women interesting. While I was at school and for the first few years out of school, I dated lots and lots of girls. I would never stay with any of them for a long length of time. I was more interested in the pursuit than settling down. As soon as a girl was interested in a long-term commitment, I would lose interest and end the relationship

Without knowing it, I had a real problem with commitment. At the time, I just thought that was normal. But later on, God revealed to me that I had an issue with a woman loving me, as I had a deep seated fear that she would abandon me, leave me or die, like my sister had. Once I became aware of this, I asked God to remove the lie. Within a short space of time, I felt healed and was ready to settle down.

A few months later I met a girl and within a few weeks, fell head over heels in love with her. She was perfect, she was beautiful, she loved Jesus, and we really got on well. I was convinced that this would be my wife and felt God confirm this for me.

A month or two into the relationship, I went on a mission trip to Mozambique. The trip had been organized by various churches, and there were many different churches represented on the trip. One day towards the end of the trip, one of the men from another church said he had a word from the Lord for me. He said, "The woman you are with now is not your wife." I thanked him for his word and walked away. I felt sure he had heard wrong; there was no possible way. Hadn't God already spoken to me?

When we returned from Mozambique, the girl ended the relationship with me. I was absolutely devastated, and I could not believe what had happened. I was angry with God and felt that He had absolutely let me down. How could this be? I thought she was to be my wife. In my mind, anyway.

Surely God was not a loving father. What kind of a father removes the hurt from my sister dying only to put me into the position of someone I loved leaving me?

I was heartbroken. Soon afterwards I heard a message at church of laying down your life for Jesus and trusting Him, that He had the perfect spouse for you. The preacher said we can trust God; He knows better than us, and He is in control and knows what He is doing. I listened to that sermon over and over for weeks as I was a broken man.

Finally after a few weeks I decided to go to England for a month or so to take my mind off things. All that I kept thinking was that God didn't love me, He was not good and He didn't care about me.

While in England I went to visit a good friend, who had been instrumental in my salvation and getting to know Jesus. He was a great person and it was the first time that I had met his wife.

The next Sunday morning when I woke up, I had said to the Lord that I was walking away from my faith that day, as I simply couldn't believe a good Father would do this to a son He was supposed to love. I had been radically saved and never for a moment thought of not serving the Lord. This morning, however, I was serious. Enough was enough, I was hurt, and God didn't seem to care.

I hadn't told my friends what was going on in me. Once we had eaten breakfast, they said I needed to come to church with them. I agreed, but in my heart had said, "Lord this is the last church service I'm ever going to."

As we arrived at the church, I started crying. We hadn't even sat down, and I was in tears. From the time I got there until the time I left, I cried. I have absolutely no idea what the service was about, what we sang or what was preached but God had met with me.

During the meeting I felt God say, "You have two choices today and they both involve death. The one option is to walk away and you will die. You have seen too much and the devil will kill you. The other option is to die to yourself and surrender to Me and trust Me."

I didn't want to go back to my old life, but surrendering everything to Jesus just seemed so overwhelming. How could I know He was good? He was asking me to trust Him with no strings attached, even if it meant that I would never marry. I would have to trust Him. So I surrendered. I knew that was the only option.

After I returned home from England, I was on an entrepreneurial TV show. Following that, I felt my ministry was to be on TV. So I decided to move up to Johannesburg and complete a television presenting course and pursue my TV career. It turns out moving had nothing to do with TV, but it had everything to do with my future.

A few weeks before I appeared on the TV program, I was at the evening service of my church in Durban. There was a girl who was sitting on her own and seemed to not know anyone. I asked a friend to ask her to come and sit with us, as she looked lonely. The girl's name was Tammie.

After the meeting, a group of people had agreed to meet at the local restaurant for a dessert and drink. I invited Tammie along. She said she would come and she followed me in her car to the restaurant. She lived in Johannesburg, around 300 miles from Durban. She was down for the weekend visiting her sick grandmother.

Once we got to the restaurant we sat down and waited for the others to arrive. But, no one else turned up and we ended up chatting until around midnight, only to be interrupted by Tammie's younger sister, in her pyjamas. She had driven through the town looking for Tammie's car, as Tammie had said she was going to church at 5pm and it was now midnight.

Tammie then left with her sister but not without giving me her phone number, as I had told her I was moving to Johannesburg in a few weeks, and she had said she would introduce me to some people.

She had clearly expressed that she wasn't interested in a relationship as she had a boyfriend at the time. I was fine with that as I wasn't looking either.

At that time I was really questioning God's love for me and as she left I said to God, "Lord, how much do you love me? Do you love me so much that you would send a girl all the way from Johannesburg to be my wife?"

It was such a random comment and I thought there was no way God would love me that much.

In the next few weeks, I moved up to Johannesburg and after a little while began to get lonely as I knew no one. I was sitting in a restaurant drinking a milkshake alone and feeling sorry for myself, when Tammie called and asked if I wanted to get together for a cup of coffee with her. As it turned out she was in a coffee shop just down the road. So, I walked straight over.

She told me she had broken up with her boyfriend and she just couldn't resist my charm. (Tammie tells me that my recollection of the day's events is slightly different to hers). But nonetheless we started dating from that day. I knew she was the girl for me, when on our first dinner date I asked if she minded if I could let out some wind. She looked at me strangely and said "I suppose so." I let one go and we both had a great laugh. Two years later we were married and lived in Durban together.

On our wedding day in 2005, as Tammie walked down the aisle, I saw her and how beautiful she looked. As she walked towards me, God reminded me of when I had asked Him how much He loved me, and if He loved me so much that He would send a girl all the way from Johannesburg to be my wife. Well, He loved me more than I could even imagine.

God is so good; His love for us shows no end. Looking back, the best decision I have ever made in my life was dying to myself and trusting God on that day in that little church in England.

I believe one of the greatest testimonies of God's love for and towards us is the spouse that He has prepared for us. They are the very expression of His love. I urge you to honour, cherish and adore the spouse God has given you.

Tammie is the perfect partner in life for me and she takes my faith in Jesus to a whole new level. There is no one on Earth with whom I would rather see the plan of God fulfilled in our lives. She is a loving, kind and mighty woman of God. I know without doubt that I would not have been able to face half the things that I have faced in my life without this wonderful woman at my side. She brings peace, calm and stability to every situation.

I want to end this chapter by imploring those who have not yet found the person God has set aside for them. Trust God as He is faithful. Surrender all to Him; He is good and will come through for you. If He did it for me, He can do it for you.

3

On a New Mission

In the beginning of 2008, Tammie and I both felt that God was changing seasons in our lives. I was previously involved in house building, but the property market had suffered heavily and building was no longer a feasible financial option for me. I was seeking God for the next opportunity that He had for us.

In early February 2008, I was thinking about going to China on a business trip to buy electricity generators and import them into South Africa. South Africa had been going through an energy crisis and electricity was being cut to homes on a daily basis.

At the time, our friend Renée was staying with us from England and we asked her to pray and tell us what she felt God was saying to us. Renée was an old friend and we trusted that she also heard God clearly. We had not told her our plans as we wanted God to confirm what we thought He had told us.

After praying she said that she didn't hear God say anything specific. Without the confirmation we were not going to move forward. I have found it's helpful with life's big decisions to get confirmation from the Lord through people you trust. We are all still learning how to hear the Lord clearly. I don't believe it's wise to change our lives on a word we think we have heard from God without a lot of confirmations from other people, those whom we trust also hear God clearly.

Having still no idea what I was supposed to do, I began seeking God more intensely. The Bible says "seek and you will find" (see Matthew 7:7), so I began to expect to find what the Lord had for us. A few weeks later I was praying in my lounge, and God spoke to my heart that we were to move to England. It was so left field that I was dumbstruck. I had no desire to move to England; I was probably one of the most passionate South African people around. I loved South Africa and always thought our future would be there.

I waited for Tammie to get home, and we discussed it. All I could envision in my mind was going for six months, taking some time away from what we had been used to. I thought during the time away God would show me a product we needed in South Africa that I could bring back, and we would be home in a few months.

Tammie, however, was not as keen as I was to go for a short period of time. She did not want to pack up our lives for just six months. After all, we had two beautiful dogs and a wonderful home which God had blessed us with. Tammie said the minimum period she would be prepared to leave for was a year. I reluctantly agreed, and I said I would submit it to the eldership at our local church first. We were not going without their blessing.

I met with one of the elders and he said he felt it was God's plan for us. Nevertheless, he would take it to the other elders, and they would pray about it. About a week later, the eldership came back to me and said they thought it was God, and we should go to England.

Tammie had a British passport, and we had been married for three years, so I applied for a spousal visa. We had a friend who had recently applied for one, so they guided us through the paperwork. We submitted the application, along with the £800 fee, and we waited.

Within twenty four hours I received a text from the British consulate in Pretoria, stating that my visa application had been processed. How good God was, I thought. We must have heard him right, and it only took twenty four hours to get a visa.

The next day I went to the visa agency in Durban to collect my passport. I opened the envelope and excitedly looked for my visa in my passport. There was nothing there, no British visa, just a consulate stamp!

I then looked at the letter attached and it read along the lines of, "We are sorry but your visa has been denied." Very little further information was given other than, "You have the right to appeal within twenty eight days but don't contact us as it may jeopardize your application." I was in shock! How could that be? I was sure we had heard God. I was bitterly disappointed.

The denial of my spousal visa had me stumped. I chatted with Tammie, and we decided we needed to appeal the decision. Two of the things they had said on the letter were that they were not happy with our finances and our accommodation once we arrived in the UK. I wasn't really sure what that meant. I phoned all the visa companies I could find in South Africa, and they all said that they did not deal with appeals. Eventually, one of the companies said the only thing they could think of was for me to contact an immigration lawyer in London and ask their advice.

I called a company in London, and they said that the appeals procedure could be quite difficult. However they could do it, but it would require £2000 before they would look into it any further. The other option would be for Tammie to move to the UK without me, and once established, she could apply for my visa, as it would be more likely to be approved. Both those options were not okay with us. We didn't want to spend that kind of money on a maybe, and we were not interested in being apart for several months. There had to be another way.

We fervently sought God but had no breakthrough. Tammie had already resigned from her job and we needed a solution. During that time our church had a leader's weekend away with a guest speaker, who was another pastor in Durban. In the middle of one of his messages he stopped and said, "Where God has called you, no one can stop you." It was just a statement spoken to everyone, but Tammie and I knew it was God speaking to us.

Once we got home it had already been about two weeks, and we still had no idea how to appeal the denial. Finally, I was on my knees praying and suddenly I thought I should contact the British trade department, tell them my story and ask them to give me the phone number of someone at the visa department who could help me. I knew the visa department had to have a phone number and there must be someone who could help us. So, I called the British trade department. I got through to a lady and explained my story to her. She said, "It is very strange that you called because I worked in the visa department for seven years and have recently moved to trade." She said luckily that day the people who worked in her department were off sick, as normally she would not be able to discuss anything like that with me. She then asked me to read to her what the denial letter said. I did so, and she promptly said I needed to get a pen. Just like that she told me, in detail, everything that I would need to get my appeal in and my application approved. God is so good!

Admittedly, it was a lot of documentation, but we knew what to do. Within a week we had everything we needed and were ready to file the appeal. We would need to drive to Pretoria to submit the application. So, we decided to drive up as soon as we could. It turns out the day we drove up was actually our wedding anniversary, but we both had been so distracted. We only realized this when we stopped for lunch on the way to Johannesburg. The plan was to stay with Tammie's mother in Johannesburg, submit our application and wait at her house for a few days until the application was approved so we wouldn't have to drive back up to Pretoria again to collect the passports. The trip is around 400 miles from Durban to Pretoria and Johannesburg is near Pretoria.

We had one day to hand in our application and then it was Easter weekend. The Tuesday after Easter weekend would be day 28, the final day we could appeal. So, we wanted to get it in before the weekend. We were about to leave for the consulate from Johannesburg when Tammie's sister said, "Perhaps, we should give the consulate a call. Their website says they are closed." We called, and it turned out they were closed. I was now really nervous. There was no room for error; we could only hand it in on the last day we had to appeal it. I've found that often, God cuts things fine. Walking by faith can be very interesting at times.

Tuesday came, and we submitted the visa. The lady had to come around the glass cubicle, as our mound of paperwork could not fit through the slot in the glass. She took our whole lives in her hands along with the original paperwork for everything we owned, including the title deed to our house and cars. She then gave us a little letter in return, which basically said, "Don't call us. We will call you and your appeal may take 6 months to process."

Six months? We couldn't wait that long. Our lives were on hold, and now neither of us was working.

We waited around in faith for two weeks in Johannesburg with no response. Finally we reluctantly decided to drive back to Durban as we needed to get back home to our dogs. All the way from Johannesburg to Durban, we were praying that God would intervene and that the consulate would call us. We would then turn around and go back and collect our documents. The call never came, and we were both very despondent.

The next day we decided to go and visit friends of ours, Shaun and Paula, who were our breakthrough couple. Every time we spent time with them, God would break through in some area of our lives.

As we turned off their street and into their driveway, my phone rang. It was the British consulate. The lady on the other end of the line said they had reviewed my appeal and that my visa had been granted. She went on to say that she would call me in the next few days to confirm when I could pick it up. Breakthrough! God is so good! Three days later she called, and we arranged for a friend to pick up the documents and ten days later we moved to England.

Upon arriving in England, we once again saw the favour of the Lord. I had received a prophetic word from a trusted friend before leaving South Africa that God was taking me from the front line and returning me to the hospital tent for some rest and recovery. This word was specific to business in that I would experience a season of not working for myself.

Within a week of our arriving in England, I got a job doing home maintenance. I started the following Monday and stayed with the company a year until the Lord called me out. Tammie also got a job in the first week, working in the travel industry where she stayed until God called her out.

Six months have turned into eight years and counting.

4

The God Who is Above a Recession

In March 2009 a very prophetic friend of mine, Wade, sent me an email with a word he felt the Lord was saying to me. Wade is a trusted friend, and the prophetic words he had spoken over me in the past had come to pass. So, I always pay attention when he has something for me.

In the email, he said that he felt like there was a change of season coming in my life in the area of work, and I would start working for myself again in the very near future. At the time I was very happy with my job, and Tammie and I were enjoying my getting paid a regular salary. Our previous experiences of working for myself had been great, but as with any business, there were ups and downs. Being employed sometimes has advantages, and I was enjoying them.

Within a week or two, things at work began to change, and all of a sudden it seemed like God's grace for the job had lifted. It was pretty much the same work but just that I didn't enjoy it anymore. I began praying and asking God what I should be doing and in what industry.

Within a few weeks it became clear I should start my own home maintenance business. During this time God also spoke to me and said He was sending me back to school, but He would pay me for it. That has turned out to be so true. As in the last six years I have been alone on different sites every day and have had the opportunity to listen to eight hours of preaching and teaching almost every day. This has been so valuable for my relationship with the Lord and my ability to hear His voice more clearly.

To be honest, I wasn't all that excited about starting a business. We were in the middle of one of the worst recessions to hit Britain in many years, and lots of people I knew were getting retrenched. Every week I was hearing of someone else I knew who was out of work. I had a job, granted I didn't like it that much anymore, but I had a job. Shouldn't I be grateful and just leave it at that? Surely this could not be God; He wouldn't make me do something like this. Wasn't God aware of the recession?

I began to pray into it some more. It became clear I would be in disobedience to the Lord if I did not step out and start my own business. I had saved up a bit of money, and Tammie and I had chatted about it. We knew if I stopped working, we would have around three to four months of savings while things got off the ground in the new business.

At the time, Tammie's salary could not support us. So, I needed to bring home income. I started doing some research on how to start this business and easily managed to find what I would need to do. God was so faithful and I began to keep a notebook next to my bed. I would wake up in the middle of the night with an idea of how I was going to do it. The name for the business even came to me one night in a dream.

Everything began falling in line and God's favour was so evident. A friend designed the logos and the website, and while she was doing that, I bought a van. It turned out the colour of the van I had bought was identical in colour to the logo she had designed for the business. God is so clever! That meant I saved over £1000 in vehicle signage, as I didn't have to get the van shrink wrapped for the sign writing that I wanted to install. I had felt from the outset that I needed to do the business with excellence. Everything I did needed to be and look very professional.

The home maintenance industry is very competitive. At first, I had no idea how to penetrate the market. God had spoken to me to base the business on sowing seed. He told me to have flyers printed and to offer any new customers a half hour free labour. With any online advertising, I was supposed to do the same thing. Galatians 6:7 tells us, a man reaps what he sows. I began to sow work and would trust God to reap work.

A month or so later the business planning was ready, and I was ready to start. I had resigned from my previous job and fully expected my business to take off from the start. I was sure this was a God thing.

The first week passed by with no calls, no emails, and no responses to any advertising I did. I was becoming despondent. What had I done? Was God really in this? Or was I just a stupid guy giving up a job in a recession? I began to seek God, and all I heard God say was, "Take the money you have saved up and give it to this person". God told me I was limiting Him because I refused to trust Him. He then gave me Proverbs 3:5-6 (NIV) which says "Trust in the Lord with all your heart and lean not on your own understanding. In all of your ways submit to him and he will make your paths straight." Wow, what a blow! Was God crazy? How could I do that? To my natural mind it made no sense, but I knew this was God. I had seen God do similar things in the past, and He had never let me down. I discussed it with Tammie, and she said we should pray about it some more and ask God for confirmation.

The following week at church one of the elders got up in the service and said that he felt God saying there was someone in the service who was limiting God because they refused to trust Him. He then read Proverbs 3:5-6 (NIV). "Trust in the Lord with all your heart and lean not on your own understanding. In all of your ways submit to him and he will make your paths straight." By this stage, I was in tears. I knew God was speaking to me and I needed to trust and obey Him.

Early the next week, I called the person to whom God had asked me to give my money and said I needed to come and see her. I put the money we had set aside in an envelope, and off I went to give it to her. God had also spoken to me in Proverbs 18:16 (NIV) which says, "A gift opens the way for the giver and ushers him into the presence of the great." God had said this gift from my business would open up a way for me and usher me into the presence of the great. I gave the money and left. She called the next day to say thank you and to tell me how significant the amount had been to her. It was exactly the amount she needed to cover rent and some other bills. She had been trusting God for breakthrough and He had broken through for her.

I was so excited and knew I had heard God. Nevertheless, the week that followed was very disheartening. In all the previous times Tammie and I had stepped out in faith in finances, we had seen immediate provision. But this time nothing seemed to change. Every morning I put on my uniform and moved into the next room, as we had only a two-room flat, and reported for duty. I was now working for Jesus and wanted to be on time for work. The only problem was that Jesus didn't seem to have any other work for me other than spending time on my knees and worshipping Him.

I was getting desperate. It was now time to call my pastor, and arrange to meet. I arrived at his house, and we spent some time together over coffee. He said that I was changing an atmosphere and I shouldn't worry. God would come through for me. Just as I finished my visit, I received a call on my business line. This was my first call from a client, and they booked in a job. Granted it was just to change a tap washer. But, it was for a charity overseen by a member of the Royal Family.

I went in and changed the tap washer, left and thanked God for my first client. On the way home, I was worshipping the Lord, and as I sat down on my sofa at home, I felt the Lord speak to me. He asked me who the highest authority in this nation was. The Royal Family, I replied. "Who did you work for today?" He asked. "One of their charities" I replied. Just then the presence of God hit me like a ton of bricks. God had ushered me into the presence of the great. Immediately, I was secure in the fact that I was a son of the Most High God, and everything would be alright. The job had very little monetary value and they never called me again, but it had cemented something in me that God was in this and it would be okay.

Not much else changed. In fact, in the natural, physical world, it even got worse. My work van blew the engine and I needed to get it replaced. A new engine would be £1300, and I now had no money. I decided I couldn't borrow money for this but instead said to God, "You have a bill. I'm doing what you called me to do, and I'm not going to worry about this anymore." I got a great paying job, to which I caught the bus, and within a week I had the money and the van was fixed. Slowly work began to come in, and the business began to get better.

I remember the first bit of money I made. The Lord spoke to me about a friend who had been out of work for a long time. God said to take that money and sow it into his life and encourage him that God would break through for him. Money can be such a powerful thing when used as our expression of God's love towards someone else. I believe true love has actions with it. It was now easier to release money, and within a short space of time, God had replaced the money and more.

About a year into the business, things were going okay but not great. I began to seek God and ask Him what I should be doing to grow the business. One day while I was praying, I heard God say that I needed to give money on a monthly basis to a friend who was studying and doing what God had told her. [Doing so would enable her to do what she was called to do and not worry about provision]. The amount God spoke to me to give her was more than I was getting paid at the time (which wasn't a lot but it was a lot to us).

I immediately said "Get behind me Satan!'" as this surely could not be God. I chatted with Tammie, and as we were leaving for a family holiday in South Africa, she said we can pray about it while away. I was under a lot of pressure and thought I must have heard wrong because I was stressed.

We went to South Africa, and while I was there, I kept bringing this word to the Lord. Every time I brought it to him, I felt Him ask, "Why haven't you done it yet?"

"Because it doesn't please me Lord," I replied.

In my mind, the main reason was that I couldn't work out how it would be possible. I was already working hard and not prepared to work harder or longer hours. All I could see was my effort; I hadn't factored in God's grace.

By the time we returned from South Africa the matter was settled in our hearts. Nothing had physically changed, but in our hearts and minds we knew what God wanted us to do, and we were going to be obedient.

Within the next week or so we had arranged to meet up with our friend and tell her the good news. We had dinner together and told her what the Lord was saying. She was blown away but after saying thank you for the love we had showed her, she said she just simply could not accept it as it was just too much money. I said no problem and in the back of my mind thought, "Thank goodness! I'm off the hook! I've done what God has asked. She said no, but I've been obedient."

A month went by, and we still hadn't paid her as she had said no. Towards the end of the second month, while we were in a church meeting, I heard God say that we were supposed to give the two months money we would have given to our friend to a church in Zimbabwe. We were already helping this church with some of the rental income that was coming in through our house in South Africa. So, it wasn't such a strange word. God had said that the church was trusting Him for a church vehicle, and that we should take this money, plus all of the money we had saved up in South Africa from the rent of our property, and give it to them.

By now this sort of giving really excited me because this was money with a mission. We were now using what Jesus had put in our hands for the building of His kingdom.

In Revelation 21, (paraphrased) it speaks of Heaven and what it looks like. The streets are paved in gold, there are mansions, and its walls and gates are covered with precious jewels. In Matthew 6:10, Jesus prayed for Heaven's will to be on earth as it is in Heaven. So often we view finance, gold and silver here on Earth as treasure, but in Heaven they're the building blocks of the kingdom. Gold is not treasure; it's pavement, and it's to be used for extending the kingdom.

It also says in Revelation 21:22 (paraphrased) that there is no temple in Heaven because the Lord Almighty and the Lamb are the temple. God is to be worshipped, not gold or money. That is what it should be like on Earth. I believe God has no problem with you having as much gold as you like here on Earth, but you had better use it to extend and build His kingdom. How foolish will we feel one day when we arrive in Heaven, and all we've ever done for God was build up a stock pile of

Heaven's pavement. He doesn't want paving; He wants you to build new mansions for more people to come and live with Him in Heaven for eternity. Use your resources to get more people saved and into His kingdom. That is its purpose; that's money with a mission.

Moving back to the story

I called the pastor in Zimbabwe and told him what we had heard the Lord say. We both were over the moon, and he was shouting and praising Jesus on the phone. Money can't buy the kind of joy we both experienced that day. He said the timing was just perfect as he was going to Durban in two weeks for a pastor's conference. While there, he would be able to collect the money and purchase a vehicle, as they had already done the research. They could get a second hand vehicle straight from Japan that was shipped regularly into Durban, bound for other African countries. Buying a vehicle like that would mean very little import duty for them and they could get a whole lot more for their money. Isn't God amazing?

The following month, the friend who had been offered the money approached us and said she had been praying about it and was asking God to provide for her. God said He already had done so and that she needed to receive what He was giving her. So, they received it, and we gave it. Sometimes money is a weapon and God can use it to bring down strongholds.

The place where our friend was working and studying was closed to the gospel. It was really frowned upon to talk about God there. Our friend had shared the testimony about what was happening with one or two people, and before she knew it, people were seeking her out and asking about this God that was paying her while she studied. We thought it was about provision, which it was, but it was actually about the gospel reaching a place that had been closed. People don't want religion; they want a real Jesus, a Jesus who is tangible in a real way, and a Jesus who loves and cares for them.

Within the same period of time, Tammie had not been experiencing breakthrough financially at work. She was working long, hard hours but had been struggling to pick up her own clients. She worked in a company and spent most of her time working for other employee's clients, for which she didn't receive commission, as was company policy. We were both getting frustrated and began to ask God what we needed to do.

A few years before in South Africa, Tammie had started to get frustrated with what she earned and finally said to God that she was going to tithe what she wanted to earn. Three months later her salary was up at the level she had tithed at. So, we knew God could break through in this current financial struggle she was facing.

About eighteen months after Tammie started working for this company in the UK, I was worshipping the Lord in my office/lounge when I heard Him say that I needed to call Tammie and tell her to transfer £200 to a friend today and in two months her salary would double. I felt the Lord say the timing was crucial and needed to be done today though. She was obedient to the word of the Lord and made the transfer. Within two days our friend phoned in tears. Earlier in the week, God had been challenging them to tithe and honour Him. By tithing they knew they would be £200 short for their bills. They had obeyed God and so had we; God had proven Himself so faithful.

I was really excited. If I had heard God correctly, I knew the rest of the word would come to pass. God is so good. As Tammie's salary was paid one month in arrears three months later her salary didn't double, it tripled. She had picked up a very lucrative client and was set to earn that kind of money every month. Praise God.

While this was all happening, we went to a church service where a guest speaker, had come to preach. He spoke on idols and said no matter how much you give, you always feel guilty that you haven't done enough. Tammie's employer was great but we knew that for her, work had become an idol and she needed to leave. We knew she had just come into a great salary. There was a temptation in our minds to just hang on a little longer, and earn some more money, so she could leave in a comfortable position financially. That was not God's plan, and we both knew it. We knew she had to resign and the time to do this was now.

Within a few days she resigned. From a natural standpoint, it was absolutely foolish. She had stood it out for two years hardly making money, and now that she had finally got her big break, she was leaving. Needless to say, colleagues in her office were confused and wanted to know why. Tammie, who is very open about Jesus, said this is what God had spoken to us and that's why we were doing it. Tammie has always been such a testimony to Jesus. Her colleagues had already seen God come through for us with a bed for which we had trusted Him. (I will tell you this story in chapter 8.)

Tammie had told me a few months earlier that she thought God was saying she needed to come and help me with my work. I literally laughed and said, "Babe I'm giving financially to this other person. I hardly get paid enough, and you want to stop work as well?" Just thinking about it stressed me out. I thought I would have to work harder in order for us to survive without Tammie's salary. But, God's grace is enough. He can make all grace abound towards you so that in all things at all time you can have more than you need (see 2 Corinthians 9:8).

After Tammie resigned, she came to help me. A few months later, we felt the season for giving to the friend was up. God had already spoken to them, and we were released from it.

The business has been a great blessing to me but has not been without its own challenges and spiritual battles. During the first year of running the business, I made a mistake on a job and drilled out a supporting ring beam on a block of flats whilst installing an extractor fan. This ended up being a serious problem. The onslaught of evil thoughts was unlike anything I had ever experienced up to that time. I was having thoughts non-stop that I would go bankrupt, the building would collapse, people would die, and I would be in so much trouble. These thoughts made it seem like there was no way out.

It absolutely rocked me. It felt like someone had taken the ground from under me. Tammie had never seen me this rocked. We knew this had to be more than just a physical thing, we had entered into a spiritual battle. Tammie and I began to seek God furiously for the solution. Tammie told me she felt that this was a spiritual giant in our lives, and it was time to cut its head off just like David did to Goliath (see 1 Samuel 17:51).

It took three days and three nights of absolute turmoil mentally when finally I heard God say I needed to read Psalm 91 in the Amplified Bible. In verse 10 it says (paraphrased) that no calamity can come near my tent. What was calamity? I looked the word up in the dictionary and saw it. It is an extreme loss or sudden disaster.

For years, every time we gave into the Kingdom of God or committed to give into His Kingdom, things just seemed to go wrong. Almost every time we gave, we would somehow lose the same amount of money we gave, in some form of unexpected disaster or expense. We eventually came to terms with it. Whatever we gave would normally cost us double.

When I read this definition, my heart went off like a rocket. I knew this spiritual giant had been in our lives for years, and it was now time to knock him down and cut off his head. I made a placard and stuck it up in our house. On it I wrote "Calamity; today (and wrote the date) we cut off your head in this house in Jesus' name. You and all your friends get out of this house forever in Jesus' name." Tammie and I prayed, took communion and stood in agreement that Jesus was our deliverer and he would provide a simple solution to the problem with the hole I had drilled, a solution we could afford to pay for, one we could just move on from and never hear anything about again.

It didn't feel like we had the victory, but we had it. We had taken it by faith. The very next day, money that had been outstanding for months was paid to us, and a solution for the hole was found. The ring beam was repaired in a week or so for a price we could afford. Since that day, we have been able to give finances freely into the kingdom of God with no repercussions.

5

Walking Through Fire

In the beginning of June 2013, I woke up in the middle of the night with the words "YOU WILL WALK THROUGH FIRE BUT YOU WILL NOT BE BURNED" ringing in my spirit. It was not audible but I could hear it deep down in my spirit. I wasn't really sure what that was all about but I was sure it was God speaking to me. I was also sure it was in the Bible but didn't know where it was. I looked it up. Sure enough it was in

Isaiah 43:2 (NIV)

"When you pass through the waters,

I will be with you;
And when you pass through the rivers,
They will not sweep over you.
When you walk through the fire,
You will not be burned;
The flames will not set you ablaze."

For most of my Christian life, I have believed that the more I walk with Jesus the easier life will be. I thought that the redemption of God would exclude me from all of life's troubles. The more I have walked with God, however, the more revelation I have got about this.

It is not the absence of fire that's the miracle; it's the walking through it and not being burned. That's the miracle. It's all over the Bible when you begin to think about it. In the story of Daniel and the Lion's Den in Daniel 6, God didn't remove the lion's den; He removed the hunger of the lions, and Daniel walked out unscathed.

If we look at Shadrach, Meshach and Abednego (see Daniel 3), God didn't exempt them from the fiery furnace; He delivered them from burning in it. Psalm 91 verse 7 (NIV) says, "a thousand may fall at your side ten thousand at your right hand but it will not come near you; you will only observe with your eyes and see the punishment of the wicked." In

Mark 4, Jesus, when on the boat in the storm, didn't stop the storm from happening (which I'm sure He could have done). He only stopped it once it had already happened, after the disciples thought they were going to die.

Look at the book of Acts. Paul was put in prison repeatedly, he was beaten, he was shipwrecked, he was bitten by a poisonous snake, but God kept delivering him, not sparing him from it. Jesus even said in John 16:33 (NIV), "I have told you these things, so that in me you may have peace. In this world you will have trouble. But take heart! I have overcome the world."

The Jesus in you overcomes the world.

Something in me began to change as God opened my eyes to the things that have happened to me in my life. A lot of what I had seen was THE FIRE, and all I could focus on was that I was going to burn. I would say things like, "Lord don't you see the fire? I'm going to burn. Please remove the fire".

But, as I began to reflect, the more I saw this awesome Jesus who had delivered me out of every situation and every fire. [More of these testimonies of walking through other fires can be found in chapter 7.] Psalm 34:19 (NIV) says

"The righteous person may have many troubles but the Lord delivers him from them all."

A few days after waking up with the words, "You will walk through fire and not be burned," I was at church and felt to share with the congregation what the Lord had spoken to me in Isaiah 43. It seemed like a supernatural faith had come upon me, and it felt like a lion was roaring in me, reminding me of what God had done in the past for me. It was quite amazing and I thought it was for the edification of the church. Little did I know that it too was God preparing me for the raging fire that was about to unfold in our lives.

A week later, I was chatting with my brother in South Africa. He was telling me he had some pain in his stomach. It seemed like indigestion and we both thought nothing of it.

The next day I was going about my work when I got a message from my mother saying my brother had been admitted to the hospital with severe pain in his stomach. The doctors were doing some tests, thinking the issue may be with his appendix.

I called him on the phone, and he said that everything was fine. He had just been in a lot of pain. I called Tammie, and we prayed for him; we left it at that.

The next day we got a phone call from him saying that the doctors had done some tests. They had found a growth on his liver on which they wanted to operate, on the following Saturday to explore further. The doctors said it looked like end stage cancer, but they couldn't be sure until they operated. So, we would have to wait and see.

My brother seemed pretty optimistic about it, and not too phased. It was just a thirty minute procedure. Afterwards, we would know more. We were obviously concerned, having already lost a sister to cancer. So, we waited in anticipation for the results of the surgery.

On the day of the surgery, thirty minutes turned into three hours and my parents began to worry. After three hours, he was released from surgery. The doctors spoke with my parents and my brother's long term girlfriend and said everything seemed okay. The abnormality they had detected was just a clump of blood vessels the size of a fist. It was nothing to be concerned about because he was probably born with it. They would just need to monitor it to see if it grew over time. It was great news, but it still didn't explain the pain.

Upon coming out of surgery, my brother was still in severe pain, running a temperature. He had to be given morphine for the pain. The doctors didn't seem concerned and said they would monitor him for the next forty eight hours to see how he got on.

I was a little concerned as it seemed no one knew what was going on. We thought about flying to South Africa to see my brother but Tammie, Hannah [my daughter], and I had just returned from a cruise with my parents and had been in Portugal a month earlier. I felt the need to work and earn some money.

On Sunday I spoke with my brother again. The doctors had told him he needed surgery again on Monday to determine why he was still in so much pain, as they thought perhaps he had an internal bleed. My brother seemed very confident over the phone. To be honest, he sounded fine, other than the occasional outbursts of pain he was having.

That Sunday we had a normal day and went to bed around 9:30pm. I couldn't fall asleep, and at 10:30pm I heard God say, "Go downstairs. You need to worship me." I knew God wanted to speak with me. So, I went downstairs and began to worship. Within a few minutes I felt the Lord speak to my spirit very clearly that

Tammie, Hannah and I needed to go to South Africa tomorrow, and that I was to lead my brother to Jesus. It was very clear. Panic tried to invade my head as I knew something was very wrong. The natural things seemed to be okay, but in the spirit realm I could sense something was not right.

I didn't tell Tammie until the next morning. In the morning I woke up crying, and Tammie knew something was up and that God had spoken to me. I told her what I had heard and she said, "If it's God, then we must go."

I had kept our pastor and key leaders at the church aware of the situation. They were praying and trusting God for breakthrough with us. You can never underestimate the prayers of the saints, as they can carry you when you feel you are barely able to stand, let alone walk.

I contacted my parents and my brother and told them we were coming. They told us not to worry and there was no need to come. This was just a small complication, which at the time is what it looked like. But we knew we had heard from the Lord and on the Monday morning, we had booked our flights and were due to fly that evening. My brother was scheduled for the operation in the afternoon.

Just before it was time to leave for the airport, I received a call from my parents. They were really upset. It seemed as if things had gone horribly wrong in the operation. While the doctor was operating through the keyhole surgery, he noticed that my brother's intestine seemed to be really close to his pelvis and that it seemed to be stuck to it. When the doctor put his instrument on it to check what was happening, he touched what turned out to be an abscess full of puss. It burst as soon as he touched it.

This is my basic understanding of the events that followed. The bursting of the abscess caused puss to spread all over the inside of my brother's body. Consequently, the doctor cut him open from his sternum to his pelvis, to take out his organs and wash them to remove the puss. If he didn't, my brother would die. The doctor had also found that my brother's colon was so infected that he decided to disconnect and bypass it, leave a hole in his side to monitor the colon and check what fluid was coming out of his body. The doctor said he was left with no option. If he hadn't done it, my brother would have been dead in a few hours. They would put my brother in the Intensive Care Unit (ICU) for two weeks to give the infection time to subside. They would then attempt to reconnect his colon. Wow, were we glad we had heard God and were about to get on the plane.

The thing that really rocked me was that I didn't know if God would restore him. God had only said to me that I would lead him to Jesus. Now don't get me wrong, heaven is a victory for any man and eternity with Jesus is better than anything else in the world. However, I was not sure if I could personally handle my brother dying and watch my parents lose another child. They had already lost one child; how could this be the will of a good God?

I remember flying to Johannesburg with mixed emotions. Yes, I was sure my brother was going to spend eternity with Jesus, but I wasn't sure how soon it would start. When we arrived in Johannesburg, I was overwhelmed with emotions and broke down at the baggage claim. I cried my eyes out, not sure if I was up to the challenge that lay ahead.

The plan was for Tammie's sister to pick us up, and we would have lunch with her. We would then fly down to Durban two hours later on the next available flight. When we met Tammie's sister, she said that my Mom had phoned, and I needed to call her straight away, as there had been further complications. My brother was due for another surgery in the next hour or so. I phoned my Mom promptly. She said I needed to speak with my brother as it may be the last time I would be able to do so. The doctors had been monitoring the fluid coming out of his side, and it was the wrong colour. If they didn't operate and fix it, he would be dead in a few hours. They didn't want to do it as he had already had two major operations in three days and it was very dangerous, but there was no choice.

I spoke to him on the phone and prayed for God's protection over him. I didn't speak to him about salvation as I didn't hear God say that. Jesus said He only did what He saw His Father do, and He only said what He heard His Father say (see John 5:19). I didn't hear Jesus say anything at the time. So, I didn't say anything about salvation. Straight after I put down the phone, I could almost hear the devil say, "You missed your opportunity. Now he will die and not be with Jesus." This doesn't help one's anxiety levels.

On the flight down to Durban, I had begun to worship the Lord with my eyes closed, and the most amazing thing began to happen. Peace like a blanket began to fall on me. I felt the Lord say that we had the final authority in this situation. We had before us life and death, blessings and curses, and we were to choose life (see Deuteronomy 30:19). Nothing had changed in the physical realm, but something in me had changed. Peace rose up in me, and the roller coaster emotions left.

When we arrived in Durban, my Dad picked us up and took us straight to the hospital. My brother was just coming out of surgery, and they were wheeling his bed to intensive care. We went up to him and got to pray for him. He wasn't with it due to the anaesthesia. He looked terrible and in a lot of pain. There was no peace.

The doctor had called in another specialist to help him with the surgery, believing the odds would be better with the two of them. They had both decided to remove his colon and install a stoma bag on the side of his stomach, which would now be his intestinal system. They said it was not ideal, but it was the best chance for his survival, and they did not have another choice. They had also said they would bypass many of his organs for a while, as they expected them to shut down. They had been exposed to a lot of air which was not good for them. They could not give us an opinion, but they did say it was his best chance to live. Only time would tell.

We were not allowed to stay long, so we went home and spent some time with my parents and his girlfriend, reflecting on what had happened.

The following day we went to the hospital to visit him. He didn't seem well at all. His oxygen levels were very low. Even with oxygen he was still not getting enough. Tam and I prayed with him and his girlfriend. Once again, I did not feel the Holy Spirit tell me to speak to him about his salvation.

There wasn't much progress that day. His kidneys began to shut down as expected. We prayed and the symptoms seemed to improve yet there didn't seem to be a breakthrough. All this time, I was keeping the church in London informed and they were amazing in lifting him and us up in prayer and contending for his healing.

The next day was terrible. Early in the morning my brother had broken down, knocked down the nurse and physiotherapist and pulled all of the intervention tubes out. The doctors had to rush to stabilise him. After some time they managed to get him stable but were unable to replace some of the devices he had pulled out, as they could only do so in surgery.

How could God still be doing something? I thought. Surely it's too late.

When the doctors saw us, they said they had done their best. They had needed to restrain him to the bed, under sedation, so that he would stay unconscious. If he were to wake up and move, he could potentially hurt himself or worse; it was just too critical.

We saw him just after they had sedated and restrained him to the bed. It was terrible. There was no peace in him. It seemed as if he was fighting the sedation with everything in him. Tam and I prayed for peace, and he relaxed a bit, but it was an awful sight.

The following day around 7pm, my brother woke up and somehow came out of the sedation. With his girlfriend at his side, he called for Tammie and me to come and pray for him. We left Hannah, our daughter, with my parents and off we went to see him. I knew something was happening, I could sense it in my spirit. I immediately called my friends in the UK and asked them to pray because I knew this was about his salvation. I didn't know if he would pass away straight after that or if God would miraculously restore him.

While we were driving to the hospital, my parents called and said he had called for them to come as well. My heart sank and all the memories of my sister's passing away began to flood my mind. Just before she passed away, she had called for us. She eventually gave up the fight and went to be with Jesus. How could we possibly do this again?

When we arrived, Tammie and I walked straight in and he said hello. The first thing I said was, "You need to give your life to Jesus". He immediately responded and said, "I know. I just don't know how."

"I'll show you," I said.

We prayed together and introduced him to Jesus. We then prayed for his girlfriend, and she too received Jesus.

Right there in the room Heaven invaded Earth. Just like that, I could sense the authority seat had changed; King Jesus had arrived. Now that he had given his life to Jesus, Tam and I began to pray and command the spirit of death to leave him as well as every other demonic power. It felt like the Lion of Judah had arisen in me, and I could tell in the spirit realm, the demonic kingdom had met the real King of Kings.

King Jesus is Lord, and when His kingdom comes, it comes with authority. Every other illegitimate authority has to leave. Within a couple of minutes, peace flooded in and the whole spiritual atmosphere had shifted. The physical world is subject to the spiritual world. When the word of God is spoken in faith, the physical world will manifest it (See Genesis 1). I declared Isaiah 43 over my brother, that even though he walks through fire, he will not be burned.

What happened over the next few days was nothing short of miraculous. The next day my brother, Grant, was up and able to sit in a chair for a few hours. His organs all began working again, and his oxygen levels returned to normal. Within three days he was discharged from ICU and put in a normal ward. Ten days later he was released from hospital.

God is so faithful. He never changes and will always deliver us. When we walk through fire, we will not be burned. This alone would be a great testimony, but that is not the end of the story. Since then my brother has undergone a reversal surgery and had his digestive system restored to almost normal. He no longer requires a stoma bag. After living together for the last thirteen years my brother, Grant, and his girlfriend, Kerry, got married in March 2014. They welcomed, Grace Lynda van der Merwe, a beautiful daughter into their family later that year. God is so good.

I have seen first-hand that we were not burned when we were put in the fire. But we needed to keep our eyes on Jesus and see what He was doing and saying (see John 5:19). We had to refuse to give in to fear, and instead allow God's perfect love to cast it out (see 1 John 4:18). God is so faithful.

Grant, Kerry and Grace Lynda van der Merwe

6

Standing for Victory

Ephesians 6:14-17 (NIV)
"Stand firm then, with the belt of truth buckled around your waist, with the breastplate of righteousness in place,15 and with your feet fitted with the readiness that comes from the gospel of peace.16 In addition to all this, take up the shield of faith, with which you can extinguish all the flaming arrows of the evil one. 17Take the helmet of salvation and the sword of the Spirit, which is the word of God."

This chapter is about standing firm when life just doesn't go your way. It's to show that God never leaves us. He is closer than we think, even when it seems like we can't see Him.

It's to show you that no matter what life throws at you, if you are prepared to stand on God's word and refuse to move, God can protect, deliver and restore you. What was meant for harm, God can make good (see Genesis 50:20).

When we walk through the Valley of the Shadow of Death, we need to make a decision to walk through it, and keep walking. We should refuse to camp there because God has a table prepared for us in the presence of our enemies (see Psalm 23).

No matter how much we feel like quitting, let's get up, stand up and hold our ground (see Ephesians 6:13). We need to get the word of God in us in such abundance that when we are squeezed, all that will come out of us is the word.

About three years ago in 2011, a very good friend, Thomas, gave me a prophetic word he felt for me. He felt that the Lord was going to teach me how to live by faith and not by feelings and emotions. He said God would teach me how to walk by faith in spite of what I saw, heard or felt.

At the time I had learned to walk by faith but somehow when things got really tough I found it difficult to see that God was good. It seemed that my relationship with God was good when life was good, but when life was rough I found myself doubting God.

Towards the end of 2011, Tammie and I found out about some good friends who were going through a really tough time financially. We had felt God say that we were to help them financially and stand with them no matter what it took and help see them through this difficult season. There are times in life when we need to make decisions that have eternal consequences. We were not sure what it would take financially to stand with them. Would it be easy to stand with them financially? Would it be comfortable for us? Could we afford it? These were all questions I began to ask myself. But would we do it no matter what? YES.

Doing what is right can sometimes be very hard and it's in times like these that we need to keep our eyes on Jesus and on His promises.

Once Tammie and I had committed to helping this couple, we realized it would take 50% of our savings to help them through this difficult season.

At the time, I seemed to be experiencing tremendous spiritual opposition in my mind and was struggling with fear with regards to standing with them. Tammie and I discussed it and we came into agreement that no matter the cost, we would do what God was asking us to do. We released the money to them and just after that life seemed to get really hard from a circumstantial point of view.

Just before Christmas 2011, an employee of ours made a mistake on a job. The mistake turned out to be somewhat of a disaster. The clients ended up having to move out of their house for three weeks and it became our responsibility to pay for their accommodation while they couldn't live in their house. I understand that naturally things happen but the timing was really strange. It seemed that the Calamity we had dealt with was trying to raise its head again.

It was a very stressful Christmas, not knowing how this issue would be resolved and if we had enough money to cover the damages. However, God is faithful and in the middle of January the issue was resolved. It did cost us a fair amount of money but we were able to cover it.

In January we went on a holiday cruise. On the cruise, I picked up an ear infection and once we returned home I was very dizzy. I found it very difficult to stand and my vision would often go blurry. The symptoms continued for many months. I would have times that my legs would become like lead and I would have to lie down. My body would become ice cold, my head would go red and my body would shiver. It was extremely unpleasant and this was happening every few days. This made it increasingly difficult to work and I began losing out on a lot of potential earnings.

I had gone to the doctor many times and Tammie had even taken me to the Accident & Emergency (A&E) on a few occasions. The doctors were great and had done many tests but they had showed nothing. From the beginning, both Tammie and I began searching the scriptures for the solution and stood on the healing scriptures we had always stood on in the past. Nothing much in the physical realm began to change though.

During that time a friend's mother had seen us at church and had said that she had had a dream about me the previous night. She had said that the dream was really horrible and in this dream she had seen a demonic buffalo that had been sent by the devil to resist me and try to push me over. She had asked God what I should do and she had felt God say that I needed to stand. I knew the dream was from God and what was happening in my body in the physical realm was a direct result of what was happening in the spiritual. My body would literally shut down. I would have to lie on the floor, my whole body shivering for minutes at a time. I knew I had to stand on the word of God but the problem was I didn't know how to do that anymore than what we were already doing. Life and the circumstances that were all happening at the same time started to become overwhelming.

One morning we woke up to someone knocking on the front door. We got up and a letter had been put through our mail box. The letter said there was a parking fine outstanding and if the penalty was not paid they would come to seize our assets. It turned out that one of our work scooters received a parking fine that had not been paid. Apparently it had now been to court and the court had decided that they were coming to seize our assets to pay for all the costs they had now incurred unless we paid the full costs in 24 hours.

We had never received any correspondence for the fine. Having no choice we paid the fine which was now over £500 only to find that a week later there was another fine on the way. We were luckily able to intercept it just in time and only had to pay around £300.

Not being well enough to work and the financial losses we had taken put a lot of strain on our finances and we were beginning to feel the squeeze. Tammie and I stood as firm as we knew how and we stood on the word of God. God had never dropped us and He wouldn't start doing it now. We began to see God's miraculous provision during this season.

The toll of the stress however, was immense and after a while I began to feel really defeated. It was during this time that I began to see my wife shine. She began to rise up in ways and stand and declare the word of God like I had never seen her do in the past. We were not going down and God would show himself strong and deliver and redeem us.

More worries

A couple of weeks after the scooter fine had arrived at our house, I was trying to add a rider to our scooter insurance policy. While I was on the phone with the insurance representative I noticed an error in the policy. The guy said he would need to look into the error and would phone me back. An hour or two later he called me back and said that the insurance company had force-cancelled my policy and I was not able to get insurance with them anymore. They had said I had lied on my policy and that was that. I was flabbergasted. I asked to listen to the voice recording, as I knew the error was on their side not mine. I had not lied, they had obviously written down the wrong information. I was told there was no need to listen to the recording as the decision had been made and that it was final. What was I to do? I couldn't run a business without being able to get insurance. This was a critical factor in me being able to earn a living.

We were due to go to South Africa for a family reunion a few days later and this needed to be sorted out immediately. By the time we were due to leave for South Africa we still had no solution and the only option I could see was to transfer the scooter out of my name and into the name of the guy who worked with me and he would insure it himself.

The day after we arrived in South Africa, I received a call from the guy who worked with us telling me that he had been in an accident and the scooter had been written off. This was all becoming too much for me and I was still experiencing major symptoms of sickness in my body. I went to see a doctor in South Africa and after a thorough examination he said he thought I had an inner ear infection. It was then too late to treat it but it was very dangerous and could result in deafness. I would have to wait up to a year for it to leave my system. This was not the welcome relief for which I was hoping. Thoughts began to play on my mind that not only was my business going down the tubes but I was also going to go deaf.

While in South Africa I chatted with a friend who was in insurance and he advised me to go the Ombudsman and lay a complaint against the insurance company. God always provides us a way out when we are in difficult situations.

When we returned to England I contacted the ombudsman and within two months the issue was resolved and the insurance company refunded my policy and the issue was sorted. God is so good. It finally looked like we were starting to see some light. It felt like we had been in a war and we had experienced heavy casualties, but we were pulling through.

A few days after returning to England, while trying to get some information for our accountants, I found out that my business owed a fair amount of money we were not aware of and the money needed to be paid in full within a few weeks. It took a couple of weeks to find out the amount that we owed and in the weeks leading up to that, I began to become overwhelmed by evil thoughts. It seemed like every minute of the day I would have thoughts of fear, calamity, disaster, bankruptcy and the likes. The God who had always delivered us in the past, now seemed to be so far away. Where was he? Why was this happening to us? Why was God allowing this? Weren't we doing what he had asked us?

I was absolutely defeated. I was trying to stand up and on His word but I was getting knocked down again and again. At the same time I also lost our major client at work who had provided me with nearly half my business revenue in the past. The fear and anxiety were immense and I would often have to phone Tammie in the middle of the day and we would pray together on the phone for ages until these thoughts would stop. Every day I would wake up with a black cloud over my head, thinking that day was going to be a day of disaster. Thoughts such as, "I am going to make a mistake at work, people will die, their house will burn down and I will be held responsible, I will end up in prison for the rest of my life, so the sooner I came to terms with this the better." Every minute of the day seemed like a struggle just to survive. I had been in some spiritual and mental battles before but never anything like this.

These thoughts were a whole new thing for me and I didn't seem to have the knowledge of the Bible on how to defeat them. There were many days that I felt like quitting and I began to ask God to take me to heaven as I couldn't live like this anymore. I needed peace and just didn't have any for nearly a year.

Going back to the money story

After a couple of weeks our accountants had a figure for us. The amount we owed was double the total money we had at the time. The payment was due in a few weeks and needed to be paid in full. What were we to do? There was only one option. We were to stand on the Scriptures and trust God. The lion in Tammie began to roar and she began to tell these mountains to move out of our way (see Mark 11:22-23). We came into agreement that God would supernaturally supply the money for this and deliver us from all that life was throwing at us. We were tithers and we were sowers. God had supernaturally supplied the Israelites with manna (see Exodus 16), he had supernaturally supplied for Elijah with the ravens (see 1 Kings 17), and Jesus had put money in the fish's mouth (see Matthew17:27). If God had done it in the Bible, then he would do it for us. God didn't lie (see Numbers 23:19) and we were choosing life (see Deuteronomy 30:19) and life abundantly (see John 10:10). God would come through.

Things began to shift and we were finally in the place where the word of God became the FINAL AUTHORITY over every situation. If the Bible said it, we received it and the physical realm would have to line up with the word of the Lord. We were no longer going to submit to what we saw, felt and thought. We were going to submit to the word of God and that was the end of the discussion. We made a decision that if we had to stand forever, then we would. We were not going to move. God was not moving, His word was unchanging and we were not moving off it. Thomas' prophetic word suddenly started to make sense. God was teaching us to live by faith in His goodness and not by feelings, circumstances, or sight.

The thoughts were still there, the sickness was still there, the financial and business issues were still there, but the victory had been won. Jesus had died on the cross and rose again for our victory and we were going to stand until the fullness of that victory was manifest in our lives. We were not taking defeat anymore. Mountain you move now in Jesus name (see Mark 11:23).

Within the time the money needed to be paid the money was there in full. God is amazing. The money came supernaturally through various sources.

The dizziness gradually began to stop and the shaking and the other symptoms stopped. Each time the symptoms reappeared we stood on the word of God, told that mountain to move and within a few minutes the symptoms would be over. Eventually they stopped altogether.

We did exactly the same thing with the thoughts. We began exercising our authority in the word and took them captive against the knowledge of God (see 2 Corinthians 10:5). It took about a year, but gradually the thoughts got less and less. Every time they tried to come back, Tammie and I would pray and declare the truth of the living word of God and the thoughts would subside until they eventually disappeared.

Our business is in the process of being restored and I have a steady influx of work.

God is good all the time and what was meant for harm God has turned to our benefit (see Genesis 50:20 and Romans 8:28). We are victorious in each and every situation. Now every day I wake up and declare the goodness of the Lord. This is the day the Lord has made and I will rejoice and be glad in it (see Psalm 118). God's goodness and mercy will follow me today (see Psalm 23).

I don't in any way believe the struggles I went through were the Lord's doing. His plans for me are good and he came to give me life and life abundantly (see Jeremiah 29:11, John 10:10). I would be lying if I said that I understood why everything happened like it did. I suppose some of it was just life going wrong, some was spiritual opposition from the enemy and some of it was just me learning how to use the word of God practically as my armour in everyday life. But nonetheless my beautiful saviour Jesus has shown himself faithful and every day we are walking more into His glorious restoration.

I believe there is nothing that can separate us from God's love (see Romans 8:38-39), and there is no situation His word cannot redeem us from. Just like in Job, when life goes completely wrong, God is the God who restores. Yes Job had many struggles but when they were all finished and done, God restored him and he received double blessing for everything he lost. In the end the Lord worked everything out for his good. Romans 8:28 tells us the same thing, if we love God all things eventually work out for our good.

So, I encourage you, when you get thrown curve balls in life, get up and stand your ground, because God is good. We are to live by faith and not shrink back (see Hebrews 10:38-39). We will not be destroyed but shall see the goodness of the Lord in the land of the living (see Psalm 27:13).

In Chapter 9 & 10, I have a lesson on the scriptures Tammie and I have stood on in the past, and that we will continue to stand on for this victory.

7

Protection, Healing, and Deliverance

God is our Protector, Healer and Deliverer and there have been many times I can remember when we have seen God's hand physically move situations in our lives. I'm sure there have been so many others that I either can't recall or didn't recognize at that moment. I know God is working all the time and His faithfulness towards us is unending.

The following testimonies are as I remember them and are in no particular order.

Boils

A number of years ago I got some sort of infection and ended up getting boils inside my nose and throat. It was very painful and I struggled with it for a few days. Then one night at Bible study, our group declared God's healing power over me and in the morning they were completely gone. They didn't gradually get better, they just disappeared.

Hijack

I remember even before I gave my life to Jesus, how God protected and delivered me. One night I went out with a friend of mine and his brother. My friend's brother was driving, my friend was in the passenger seat and I was in the back seat. We stopped off in a fairly undeveloped area in Durban to pick up another friend. As we pulled into the driveway in the middle of nowhere, we rang the intercom. We were waiting for a reply and to be let in through the automated gate, when my friend's brother noticed someone standing next to the driver's window. I also saw him and in the dark we could see a guy standing near the window with what looked like an AK47 in his hands. We shouted at him, then noticed another man with a similar weapon standing at the passenger window. Panicking, my friend's brother threw the car into reverse gear. The reverse lights lit up and behind us was another man with a gun. By now we were all gripped by fear and my friend's brother stalled the car.

Looking back at what happened next was miraculous – the protection of God. Time seemed to stand still and in what seemed like a split second, the driveway gate opened, we restarted the car and drove through the gates towards the house. The men with the guns just stood there, they didn't shoot, they didn't follow us; they just disappeared in the rear view mirrors.

Guns

There was another time after I had been serving God for a few years where I experienced His power in a similar way. I was working down near Durban, fibre glassing a swimming pool. I was working with a guy called Bongani. While sanding the swimming pool, we ran out of sanding disks. I told Bongani I would just pop out to the hardware store down the road and would be back shortly. Fifteen minutes later I drove back down the long driveway and instantly started crying. The Holy Spirit was all over me and I didn't know what was going on. At the end of the driveway I saw two men who were at the gate looking for work. They saw me, waved hello and walked past the van, back down the driveway and back onto the street. In South Africa having people come to the gate looking for work is fairly normal, so I didn't think anything of it and they looked fairly harmless. But, something was going on in my spirit that I couldn't shake. I arrived at the driveway gate and rang the intercom. The driveway gates opened and I began to drive through. The only way I can describe what happened next was that the Holy Spirit arrested my body.

I could only get half way through the gate and could not drive any further. I opened the van window and shouted for Bongani, who was only a few metres away, but behind the swimming pool fence, so I couldn't see him. There was no reply. Something was wrong but I had no idea what it was. I put the van in reverse and sped down the driveway into the street. I phoned Tammie and she asked what was wrong. Still crying I said I had no idea but I knew something was very wrong. We prayed and asked God for wisdom, peace and protection over me, Bongani and the cleaner who was also on the property.

Not sure what to do, Tammie suggested that I call the police and tell them I thought that something was wrong at the property. I tried to call them but unfortunately in South Africa calling the police can be quite fruitless. They said that if I didn't know what was wrong, they couldn't help and they were not allowed to call mobiles so they would not be able to call me back when a van became available, as the one they had was busy.

Not to criticise the police service in South Africa but people who have lived in South Africa will understand that that sort of response can be fairly normal. About fifteen minutes went by and in the meantime I had driven around the block out of view of the property. I called Tammie back and said I was going to drive past the property again and see if anything had changed in my spirit.

As I drove back I saw three men walking down the street with guns in their hands. They were around a hundred metres in front of me walking away from me so they did not see me. I stopped the car and waited for them to turn the corner and then they disappeared. About two minutes later, private security vehicles began to arrive on the scene. After chatting with me, one of the vehicles went in pursuit of the men with guns and the other sped up the driveway towards the house. I just waited there and let them do their jobs. I'm no hero and was very comfortable sitting in my van until I received the all clear. Moments later the security guard signalled that everything was okay and that it was safe for me to return to the house.

When I got to the top of the driveway I saw Bongani and the cleaner. They began to tell me what had happened. Bongani described how just after I had left three men had arrived with guns and held a gun to his and the cleaner's head. They had said they were not here for them; they were here for the "umlungu", which means white man in Zulu. When they saw that I had already left, they began to get upset and after a few minutes got spooked and left. During that time, the owner of the property had phoned home and because the cleaner had not answered became suspicious and phoned the private security company, who arrived upon my return to the property. It was a really scary experience but God had miraculously intervened, delivered and protected us all.

Accident

One day I was driving down to the beach front to attempt to go spear fishing with a friend for the first time. It was raining quite a lot. As I came around the corner on the motorway I noticed that all the lanes were blocked up and there had been an accident in front of me. I swerved my car as I was certainly going to hit the car in front. In the wet I lost control of the car and I remember shouting out, "THANK YOU JESUS, THANK YOU JESUS." My car spun around and around and then went off the road and collided with the barrier on the edge of the motorway. The impact destroyed the whole right hand side of the car. As the car came to a stop I was still shouting, "THANK YOU JESUS." Just then, I saw car after car crash into the collision that I had just avoided. I was still in harm's way as my car had finally come to a stop halfway on the motorway and halfway on the hard shoulder at a right angle to the oncoming traffic with the driver's door facing the traffic. I knew I had to get out. I tried to open my door but the impact had crushed the door and I couldn't open it. I climbed across into the passenger seat and got out through that door which opened fine. I ran to the edge of the hard shoulder to safety.

Once I got clear I could see car after car crashing into the pile of vehicles that I had swerved to avoid. I counted five in all while I was there. I don't know if anyone was killed that day but God had delivered and protected me and I walked out without a bruise or a scratch. For me, it was a living example of Psalm 91 in action. Particularly the part where it says 1000 may fall at your side 10 000 at your right hand but it will not come near you.

Blood Pressure

A year or so before Tammie and I moved to the UK I went through a period of many months where I suffered with extremely high blood pressure. It profoundly affected my body and I had great difficulty working. There were many days that I was unable to work or do much of anything as I was so dizzy and found it difficult to stand up and walk properly. There were many times I struggled to read or see properly as my vision would go blurry for minutes at a time. On a few occasions Tammie rushed me to the hospital because I thought I was having a heart attack. I had been to see various doctors and they had put me on blood pressure pills. They said I was overweight and I needed to exercise and lose some weight. It was pretty unpleasant and it sounds stupid but every day that I woke up alive I was excited as I wasn't sure I was going to wake up every day.

I believe the enemy had me convinced he was killing me and from the natural symptoms he seemed to be doing a half decent job. We had prayed and asked God for breakthrough many times and stood on whatever scripture we could find. But for months, no breakthrough came. I remember being in a prayer meeting at church one night and as I was standing at the back of the meeting, I had this strange feeling I was going to die that night. It was really scary and seemed so real in my head.

I've always felt, since I got saved, that I was called to ministry. At that moment in my mind I thought perhaps my ministry was that God was going to raise me from the dead. I realized I was at the back of the church and quickly made my way to the front of the church. If I died at least I had a good chance of coming back from the dead. After all wasn't the front of the church where "real people of faith were"?

When I got to the front I was given the microphone and to be honest I have no idea what I shared. I finished sharing, realised I was not dead and then returned to the back of the church. Just then our pastor left the front of the church, which he never did while leading a meeting, and came to the back of the church and prayed for me. I felt fire go through all of my body and the heat I experienced was immense and really tangible.

I was convinced God had healed me, so the following day I returned to the doctor to have it medically verified. When I got to the doctor I explained to him what had happened to me the night before and that my pastor had prayed for me and that I had felt fire through my body, the whole story. He looked at me really strangely.

"I don't believe in that," he said as he began to take my blood pressure. It was higher than ever and he said I needed to go on a 24-hour monitoring period with a blood pressure machine attached to me taking my blood pressure every ten minutes so they could see what was going on. He said that it was extremely abnormal for a guy my age to have such high blood pressure.

I knew that this was also spiritual and not just natural but I just didn't know how to get free.

Then one day, a friend who rented a flat we owned, said her mom, Peta, was coming to town and she dealt in deliverance ministry. She asked if her mom could pray for me. I was a little apprehensive at first as I didn't know her mother and I felt I was dealing with enough issues. I didn't need any more. After all I was a Christian and surely didn't need deliverance? Also wasn't deliverance weird and spooky? What if she prayed for me and things got worse? The things I had heard of deliverance and things I had seen in movies seemed like a massive fight between good and evil and it always seemed to be a toss-up as to who would win.

After weighing up my options, I reluctantly agreed. I would take my chances. I was pretty spiritually aware, and I would tell her to stop if I felt something she was doing was not in the Bible or didn't sit well with me. Tammie was also quite nervous but we prayed for God's wisdom and leading and protection. Like I said, the deliverances that I had heard of in the past were pretty full on and we were fully expecting a scene from some horror movie.

What happened that night was really different and actually really pleasant. Our friend and her mom arrived at our house, and we all said hello and made some small talk. Her mom then said, "Just relax, it's not going to be hectic. We are just going to pray and ask Jesus what's going on here and we are going to ask Him to set you free. Let's make some coffee and let's begin to pray."

Tammie sat on the sofa with her feet up, making sure she didn't catch any of the demons that might float past her on the floor. It sounds funny now but at the time we were both pretty nervous. Once we started our coffee, we started praying.

After a few minutes Peta asked me to stand, laid hands on me and said, "I feel like the devil is trying to suffocate you and he has placed a snake around your heart."

This is what it looked like in the spirit. Tammie and I pretty much saw the same thing in our spirits. It's hard to describe, you couldn't physically see it but somehow God opened our spiritual eyes for a moment to see it, if that makes any sense. I'm sure in the natural physical world it was far less dramatic. Peta reached into my chest (in the spirit), placed her hand around my heart, pulled and she said, "Devil, I command you to loose yourself off Byron and come off him in Jesus' name."

Instantly I breathed in and it felt like a huge weight had been lifted off me. Immediately the dizziness I had experienced for months stopped and I felt completely normal. In her hands I could almost see this snake and she threw it off and commanded it to leave and

never return in Jesus' name. By this time
Tammie had crawled a little higher on the
sofa. Now Peta definitely had my attention
and my confidence in her ability grew
substantially. Other people had prayed for me
for months with no results and here in fifteen
minutes I was free. I was suddenly far more
aware that there is a very real spiritual realm
out there, one which I didn't know much
about, even as a Christian. Peta carried on
praying and said she felt there was more. Who
was I to argue? So, we had another cup of
coffee and she carried on praying. The next
minute she asked whether I suffered from any
fear. OH YES!!

Since the time I was a little boy, I had not
been able to sleep properly and used to have
nightmares almost every night. From a young
age I couldn't sleep in my room and I used to
end up in my sister's room most nights as I
was so frightened. Looking back now, Lynda
had Jesus with her and that's probably why I
could sleep in her bedroom. After I got saved
the bad dreams intensified and I couldn't sleep
without having some preaching on. I used to
dream of evil looking things flying through the
windows all the time coming to kill me.

A friend of mine chatted with me and he said
that where there is light, darkness cannot be.

So, if Jesus is the light in me, then when the physical light goes out at night Jesus' light is still on in me. In theory, this is great and I absolutely believe that to be true. At the time though my light seemed a little low and the best way to keep the light shining was to listen to preaching. I still listen to preaching day and night but now I don't listen because I have to, I listen because I want to listen. When Tammie and I got married she found it very unsettling as I very seldom slept peacefully and I would often wake her to pray for me and declare God's peace over me. She also would never walk into the room unannounced if she went to bed after me as she knew if I saw her I would jump up and be ready to fight. It was so bad that I was afraid to sleep out in other places in case the dreams got worse. Most nights I was a prisoner in my own bed.

So, when Peta asked if I suffered from fear, I knew a little something of what she was talking about. She said she felt God wanted to show me when this fear arrived and that God would remove this root from my heart that night. I had tried for years to get rid of this fear but with little victory. That night within a short space of time God had showed me the root of when this fear started.It was just a little statement that someone had made to me that had caused fear to come in. All that was needed was for me to repent of believing a lie. I asked God to remove the fear and I told the fear and the devil to leave me alone.

To be honest it didn't seem very spiritual. I didn't see any snakes as before or even feel anything different. She also prayed that God would close my spiritual eyes to the enemy. She prayed that I would discern his strategies but would no longer see his works in the spirit.

In the days, weeks, months and years after that night the dreams have pretty much stopped and I very seldom have nightmares anymore. Praise God for His deliverance.

I still listen to preaching almost all day and I can count on my hands the days I have not gone to sleep without listening to preaching, but now it's because I really enjoy it and it is no longer a matter of survival. I will forever be grateful to Peta for surrendering her whole life to Jesus and allowing Him to work through her. Since that night I have decided to pursue Jesus relentlessly so that I too may be one of those people to whom He gives the keys to unlock the strongholds of the devil and set people free into the freedom that Jesus paid for them.

Followed at night

Another small testimony was that one night
Tammie and I were sure we had been followed
home. We were still living in South Africa at
the time. Every turn we made the car behind
us made also. We were concerned so we drove
straight past our house and the car still
followed us. So, we phoned the private security
company and they said their vehicle was
literally on the road next to ours and they
would come and escort us home. Within
minutes the security car arrived and the car
behind us turned down another road and was
gone. God always protects.

Where's the runway?

Tammie is originally from Johannesburg and
all her family live there. We lived in Durban at
the time and would travel up to Johannesburg
every two months or so to visit her family. We
used to drive but every time we drove there
seemed to be weird things that would happen.
We got stuck in hail storms, and once the road
we were on got struck by lightning and fire
shot across the road. Another time we got
stuck in torrential rain going through a
section of road works when the car on the
other side of the road spun out of control and

headed straight for us. I luckily saw it in time and managed to give Tammie who was driving enough warning to move out of the way.

We then decided we were not going to drive to Johannesburg anymore because it was just too hair-raising. So, we decided to fly. The only issue was that fear was so rampant in my life at the time that I was afraid to fly and I would have dreams of the plane crashing every time we were due to fly.

Most flights I spent with my hoodie over my head or my eye patch on and my mp3 player in my ears so I would not see what was happening around me. Tammie on the other hand loved flying and weirdly enough there was a time in my life where I loved flying too. Just during this season I certainly didn't.

I remember one particular flight to Durban from Johannesburg. It was raining very heavily and there were storms en route. You know those moments, when the captain comes over the PA system and says, "Ladies and Gentleman, unfortunately we will not be serving any refreshments this afternoon as there may be a little turbulence during the flight. There is a storm en route so it might be a little bumpy. Cabin crew, please remain in your seats."

Now that's great news to someone who already doesn't want to be on the airplane. True to form I had my hoodie over my head and my earphones in, worshipping my way through the fear. The flight was bumpy but that wasn't the problem. The problem was that when we arrived near Durban the pilot couldn't seem to land on the runway and kept pulling out of the final approach each time we were about to land.

The plane's engines would go right back and the plane would nose dive quite steeply and the next second, there would be a huge acceleration and we were thrust back into the air. The plane then circled and started the whole procedure again and again. It had been around one hour forty five minutes on what was meant to be a fifty minute flight and even Tammie was starting to get nervous.

I was sitting under my hoodie asking God to deliver us, when it suddenly dawned on me that when Jesus and His disciples were in the boat and the huge storm came up, the disciples were freaking out but Jesus was sleeping (see Matthew 8:24). He simply got up rebuked the storm and that was that. I had a revelation right then and there that we are not subject to fear and natural situations. They are subject to the Jesus inside of us. I looked at Tammie and we came into agreement and commanded that airplane to find the runway and land safely in Jesus' name. Peace flooded my body and it was hardly 30 seconds later and the plane touched down on the runway.

It was only after we got off the airplane that we realized how severe the weather was. There were gale force winds outside and it was difficult to walk, never mind fly.

Fire

In 2013 we went on a cruise with my parents. We had a great time and loved every minute of it. The second to last night Tammie had a dream. In the dream she saw the ship we were in sinking, but that we ended up being okay. There had been a gas explosion in the funnel of the ship that had caused it to sink. She was really freaked out by the dream and woke up asking me to pray for peace. At the time she didn't tell me the details of the dream because she knew it probably would have terrified me also and I would have spent the whole night praying.

On the last night of the cruise, we went to bed at around 10pm. I had my earphones in and was listening to preaching. I fell asleep but the preaching was still playing when Tammie woke me up and said, "Babe, the fire alarm just went off. The captain has just come over the PA system and said there is a fire on board but not to panic and remain in our rooms."

My heart went off like a rocket. WHAT? Tammie then told me the details of her dream the night before and suggested that perhaps it was time for us to pray. I began praying. I prayed, shouted out loud and declared God's authority, including the entirety of Psalm 91 over everything I could think of.

I then phoned my parents; their response was to go back to sleep, since the Captain had told everyone to stay in their rooms. I phoned the reception and asked them if this was a drill. "I'm really sorry, but it's not a drill. There is a fire on board and it's serious, but it's safest for you to remain in your cabin," she said. I opened our cabin door to find all the other doors open as well, with most people staring outside looking down the corridor to see if they could see anything. A few of them had on their life jackets as well. I went back into the room and said to Tammie that I thought we should get our life jackets ready and pack a blanket or two in our back pack. It was our last night on the cruise and they had already taken our bags and all our clothes. So, we had very little to pack in the bag in terms of warm clothes. It was not dying that concerned me; it was floating in the sea for a few days in a life boat that didn't excite me. I remember that all I could think was, "If these guys charge me for the water out of the mini-bar, I'm going to be furious."

Tammie and I came into agreement, as in Matthew 18:19 that the ship would sail on its own with no fire back into Port. I also texted a friend and asked him to pray and stand in agreement with us. After that Tammie said she was tired and going back to sleep. She had peace that God would protect us. Hannah, who was seven months old, slept through the whole thing.

My mind was racing and there was no chance I could sleep as we still didn't know what was happening. Finally, after another hour, the captain came over the speaker system and said there was a fire in the gas burner in the funnel of the ship but they had managed to contain it and everything was okay. We could all go back to sleep.

I went and looked outside our cabin and saw smoke in the corridor and could almost hear the devil say, "You see, it's not over yet. The captain is lying to you; he's pulling a Costa

Concordia on you" (the cruise ship that sank the year before).

One thing I will give the devil is that he's a liar and a good one at that. The Bible says he's a liar and the father of them (see John 8:44), but that's just it, that's all he has, he's a liar and what he says is not the truth.

The ship then sailed unhindered and arrived safely into Port the following morning. On the way down to the disembarkation point we overheard some people talking, saying they were on the Lido deck (open top deck) when it happened and they saw smoke and flames billowing out the top of one of the ship's funnels. We were relieved to be getting off the ship but once again our faithful God had delivered and protected us.

Blood

In 2012, when our daughter Hannah was born, I was going through a tough time with evil thoughts (as explained in Chapter 6). Hannah's birth and Tammie's labour were pretty standard but just after Hannah was born I had this thought that kept coming. The enemy was trying to kill Tammie and she was going to die. It really freaked me out. I called a friend and they prayed with me. They declared God's blessing and protection over all of us. Everything seemed fine and we returned home. Tammie was recovering well and we were adjusting to having a new born baby for the first time.

Three weeks into her recovery, Tammie developed a complication from giving birth. One day I had to call an ambulance and they took her off to the hospital as she had excessive bleeding. The whole day and night they struggled to control the bleeding and the next day, after they had done a scan, they discovered there was still some placenta left behind in her womb which was bleeding. My mind began to panic. How this could be? Wasn't God bigger than any natural, physical thing and any attack from the enemy? I didn't understand but knew it was crucial to agree with Heaven and not with what was going on here on Earth. Jesus had paid the price for Tammie's total healing (see Isaiah 53:5, 1 Peter2:24). Now we had to stand in faith and believe that His blood and the stripes that He had endured were enough for us.

I knew our words needed to line up with God's words and that and that alone was what we were to hold on to. But in a situation like that, it is easier said than done. Everything within me wanted to panic and fear but even though I was an emotional wreck, I knew I had to submit to God and resist the devil. This situation and the devil would have to flee from us (see James 4:7). In circumstances like this I'm learning it's not how I feel that's important, it's what I believe in spite of what I feel that is important.

The doctors had scheduled Tammie in for a procedure that evening to get rid of the remaining bit of placenta and stop the bleeding. You can never underestimate the power of people praying for you when you are feeling defeated and everything looks like it is not going the way you know God's word has promised. I sent everyone I knew who had faith and would pray a text and asked them to stand in agreement with me for Tammie's total healing, protection and deliverance. God was true to His word, everything went smoothly and today she is completely healed.

Skin Cancer?

A few years ago, Tammie had a growth on her lip which seemed to be getting bigger. It got really hard and then popped. We began to feel that something was not right with it. She went to the doctor a few times only to have him tell her not to worry and that it was probably nothing. Something didn't sit right in our spirits, however, and we felt we needed to pursue it further. Tammie was referred to a skin specialist. Upon examination the specialist said she thought it was skin cancer and it needed to be removed. They scheduled in an appointment at the local hospital to remove it. We felt to tell very few people as we knew it was critical to speak life over the situation.

Proverbs 18:21 NIV says "the tongue has the power of life and death, and those who love it will eat its fruit". We ended up only telling a few people, who we knew would stand in agreement with us for her total healing and complete deliverance.

Tammie and I decided to write out a prayer of petition to the Lord (see Philippians 4:6) and bring His word to His remembrance and sign and date it, that on that day, she had received her total healing and deliverance from any form of cancer. Mark 11:23 says you need to believe you receive when you pray. That word "receive" in Greek can also mean "to take". So, we took our healing.

The growth began to shrink significantly but did not disappear. Tammie had the remainder of it cut out and all the tests came back completely clear. God is so good all the time; He never fails. I'm not saying she had skin cancer but I am saying she definitely doesn't have it anymore. Praise God.

There have been many other occasions when God has protected, healed and delivered us and each day that goes by we experience more of His goodness. God is a good God and He is here to protect, deliver and heal you. The interesting thing I have learned is that the Bible says in Isaiah 54:17a NIV that "No weapon forged against you will prevail." It does not say that the weapons will not be formed. At times they are forged against us but if we agree with God and His word, when all is said and done these weapons cannot prevail.

Most of the time when God has protected, delivered or healed us, I have not felt anything special--no huge fire, no visions. On the contrary, I have felt vulnerable and exposed and often scared. But, God has always been faithful and His word has never failed us. He has come through every time, even those times when things didn't turn out like we expected.

So, I encourage you. Stop waiting to not feel fearful. Trust God to heal, protect and deliver you. Believe you have received when you pray

(Mark 11:23) and take hold of your deliverance by faith. If God has done this for us, He can do it for you. Revelation 19:10b (NIV) says that "For the testimony of Jesus is the spirit of prophesy." Let what Jesus has done for us begin to prophesy over your situation - that the same God who delivered us is in you and is able to deliver you.

If you know Tammie and I, you will know that there is nothing special about us. We aren't specially chosen by God or anything like that. God's word is available to anyone and everyone who will take Him at His word. So I urge you to begin to take His word as the truth and the final authority in your life, no matter what it looks like or feels like. He is the same yesterday, today and forever. Trust Him, stand on His scriptures and you can begin to see supernatural miracles as well.

TESTIMONIES *of a* GOOD GOD

8

Supernatural Provision

Over the years God has shown Himself so faithful in our lives and we have experienced many acts of His supernatural provision. I wanted to share a few of them with you.

Plane ticket

In 1998, a year or so after I gave my life to Jesus, I was reading a book about a great man of faith. In the book he was telling of how God had moved mountains for him and how he had seen God do impossible things. One of the things that really stuck with me was when he said that when we ask God for something we

need to be specific. We need to stick to what we are believing God for, and not waver.
Well I took this to heart.

A friend of mine was getting married in Cape Town in early January and had invited me to the wedding. It was around July and I figured I had plenty of time to earn the money for the two hour plane ticket to Cape Town. I excitedly agreed to go.

I asked God for a plane ticket to Cape Town and began to believe him for money to attend the wedding. I was a student at the time and my income was very low, only earning money waiting tables at a local restaurant.

The months rolled by and by the end of December I still had no money to purchase a plane ticket. In early January my friend called and asked if I was still coming to the wedding. I was put on the spot, I had not seen the provision needed to get there but I had asked God for a plane ticket and the Bible says, "Ask and you shall receive" (see Matthew 7:7). I replied, "Yes of course I'm coming." My mind began to panic. I had now firmly committed to something I knew I had no natural provision for getting there. The wedding was on a Friday and at the beginning of the week there was still no sign of a plane ticket. I began to ask

God what I needed to do. I looked through the scriptures around faith and all I could find was in James 2:17, which says that faith without deeds is dead.

In my mind I figured I had done nothing to show God that I was serious about this and had not done any deeds in response to my faith. I had an idea. What would I do if I had a plane ticket? I would go to the airport and use my ticket.

So, on Tuesday morning I packed my bags and headed to the airport. I had enough money to pay for parking for a few days and I decided I would park my car, take my bags and go and sit in the airport until my ticket either fell out the sky or someone gave it to me. I figured God could do anything. I had read about what God had done for other men and I knew God was no respecter of persons but he does respond to faith.

So, there I was, sitting in the airport, bags at my side waiting for my ticket. Hour after hour went by and still no ticket. Then I spotted a friend's grandmother. She knew me and she came over to say hello. I knew she was a Christian and thought that this must be my God appointment. She must be the person with my ticket. I was certainly not going to ask her for the ticket, so I just waited for her to say something. When she got to me, she said hello and asked where I was going. "I'm off to Cape Town." I said. "That's great! I believe the weather's really nice there this time of the year. Have fun," she answered and then she walked off. My hopes of a ticket seemed to disappear out the airport as she left.

I waited for a few more hours and then, bitterly disappointed, eventually took my bags and headed for my car to return home. I cried in the car all the way home. I was sure God could do the impossible but could not understand why He had not done it for me.

That night I went to the Bible study group I attended. I was still feeling disappointed and so I decided to share what had happened with our group. After sharing, a couple of the guys laughed and said I was crazy because God doesn't work like that.

Another couple at the meeting was also going to the wedding and they were driving down to Cape Town the following day. They said that they had plenty of space in their car and did I want to go with them? I thanked them for the offer and was about to say yes, when I felt God speak to me in my spirit saying, "You asked me for a plane ticket, not a lift."

This sounds great in theory but here I had a physical way of getting to the wedding. In raw faith (or stupidity) I thanked them for the offer and said I had asked God for a plane ticket and that's what I was going to trust Him for. If He came through that would be great but if He didn't, I was prepared to look like a fool. Everyone at the home group laughed and said I was crazy. From a natural point of view I probably was, but I had heard about the God of the impossible and wanted to see Him in action.

The next morning I woke up and was just lazing around the house. The next minute my phone rang. On the other line a lady said, "Hello, are you Byron van der Merwe?"

"Yes," I replied.

"Please get a pen because here are your flight details to Cape Town," she said.

Wow! I was in awe of God's goodness! It had been a long haul, but the day before the wedding God had come through. I got the ticket details and headed back to the airport, this time with my ticket confirmation. God is so good. I stayed with some friends in Cape Town and when I arrived at the wedding the following day, we all had a great time. I subsequently found out who God had used to provide the ticket, but God had supernaturally provided.

All our money

A few years ago, while still living in South Africa, I was chatting with some friends who were going through a rough time financially. Without discussing it with Tammie or asking the Lord, I just told them that we would meet their needs for the month. Later I phoned Tammie and told her what I had done. We ourselves were not in a great position financially at the time but she said okay, and that she would get on board.

A few days later our friends came back and told us what they required. It wasn't a massive amount of money but it was everything I had in my business. Giving this money to them would mean we would not have enough money to meet our own needs for the month.

I was a bit overwhelmed and began to think of a way to get out of it. After all, God hadn't spoken to me or anything; it was all me. Surely I had a responsibility to my wife to put our family first? If there was any leftover then that's what we would give. I began seeking the Lord. I was reminded of Matthew 6:33, where it says "But seek first his kingdom and his righteousness, and all these things will be given to you as well."

What was the kingdom? God so loved the world that He gave his only Son. Jesus was prepared to give everything for me, so how come I was struggling to give everything to Him? Surely putting others' needs ahead of mine was the Kingdom? God began to speak to me and said, "Men of integrity keep their word." Right then I knew that even if we sank, we were going to put God's Kingdom first and we would release the money. Jesus is not sinking and as long as I kept my eyes on Him we could not go down. He knew our needs and there was grace available to make all things abound to us at all times (see 2 Corinthians 9:8). Tammie and I came into agreement and we released the money. It left us with the equivalent of ten pence in my account three days before all our bills were due.

Just then the supernatural began to happen. Overnight, three clients to whom I had sent quotes made the decision to go ahead with the work and paid their deposits. When I woke up in the morning there was the equivalent of

£3000 in my account. God had supernaturally provided. We had more than enough to pay all the bills and still had plenty left over. God is so good.

Our Faith Bed

About a year after we moved to England, we were given a second-hand bed by some friends. The bed was a blessing, but it was really small and very uncomfortable and most mornings I had to take ibuprofen as my back was so sore. I was running a business and we had more than enough money to buy a new bed. Tammie had said she would like to grow her faith and see God supernaturally provide us with a new bed. She didn't want us to buy one or have it come through some form of finance that we could make; she wanted to sow a seed and see God bring in the harvest. I reluctantly agreed as I figured this may take some time to come to pass and my back was sore.

Standing in faith for something does not always happen in the time frame we would like. What if this took a year or two to come? Was I prepared to wait for God? Surely it would just be quicker and easier to buy a bed with the money God had already blessed us with?

We finally came into agreement for a new bed. We have learnt in the word that nothing happens without a seed (see Mark 4:26-29, Galatians 6:7). Friends of ours had spoken to us about some pillows they wanted, but had held off buying them as the pillows were expensive. Tammie and I decided to buy them pillows for their bed as our seed for our bed. Just like a farmer plants a seed expecting a harvest. We planted a seed of faith that was for someone's bed, trusting God that the seed would grow and we would bring in a harvest of a new bed.

We sowed the seed and time began to go by. Month after month passed and there was still no sign of a new bed. During that time we had even seen a few trucks arrive with beds in them at our block of flats, and we got so excited thinking that perhaps this was our bed. Each time though, the delivery man never pushed our buzzer to get in. I began to get frustrated and even contemplated ordering a bed and having it delivered without Tammie knowing. The only problem was that she handled all the finances and not only did I not even know how to get onto internet banking to do it, Tammie would definitely notice money going out of our account. Tammie had also told her colleagues at her office that we were trusting God for a new bed, so our hands were tied there. Occasionally some of them would come to visit and if they saw a new bed they would ask if God provided it. It wouldn't be a great testimony if He hadn't provided it supernaturally and we had bought it ourselves.

So, we continued to wait and I kept taking ibuprofen. About eighteen months after we had initially asked God to provide a bed and sowed our seed, we received an envelope at church. In the envelope was £1000 and inside there was a note, saying "This is for your house." Tammie and I both immediately knew this was for our bed. God had supernaturally provided. We went and bought the bed we wanted and had money left over to buy all the linen and duvets for the bed. God had provided over and above for what we had asked (see Ephesians 3:20).

As soon as the bed arrived, Tammie went and told her office. What a testimony! Most of them were shocked and didn't know God could do miracles. God is so good.

Baby Time

In 2012, while we were going through the troubled times discussed in Chapter 6, we found out that Tammie was pregnant with our first child. We were really excited, but from a financial point of view we were going through really difficult times. I began to get concerned about how I was going to provide for my growing family. I soon began to realise that the problem was not with God, it was me. I had taken on the role of the provider, when actually that is God's role.

As a Christian I had surrendered my life to Jesus; He was the head of my house hold, and He was the provider. I work for Jesus; I don't work for myself and ask Jesus to bless it. He is the source, not my ability.

I began to get a bigger revelation of this truth and we began to cast the care of this over to God (see 1 Peter 5:7). God cared for us, we were sold out and obedient to everything we heard him say and He would provide. Having little money to provide for our new baby's toys, clothes or any of the other things required, we asked God to supernaturally provide for Hannah, our unborn child. Psalm 139 told us that God had knitted Hannah in Tammie's womb and therefore He was aware of every natural limitation we had and He was able to overcome them. Jesus prayed in Matthew 6 that God's will be done on Earth as it was in Heaven. In Heaven there is no lack of provision, so by faith we could believe God for no lack here in our lives on Earth. Matthew 18:18 says that (paraphrased) whatever has been loosed in heaven can be loosed on earth and whatever has been bound in heaven can be bound on earth.

There was provision in Heaven and so we could loose it on Earth in our lives. Lack, shortfall and poverty were bound in Heaven so we could bind its works in our lives on Earth. Read Revelation 21 and 22 where it speaks of Heaven; there is no lack there. Psalm 23:1 says, "The Lord is my Shepherd, I lack nothing." Psalm 34:10 says, "The lions may grow weak and hungry, but those who seek the Lord lack no good thing".

2 Corinthians 8:9 told us that though Jesus was rich, he became poor, so that by his poverty we might become rich. Colossians 1:13 told us that we have been delivered out of the devil's dominion and into God's dear son's dominion. In God's Kingdom there is no lack.

Galatians 3:13a says "Christ redeemed us from the curse of the law." Deuteronomy 28 told us that lack was under the curse. Deuteronomy 30:19 says "This day | I call the heavens and the earth as witnesses against you that I have set before you, life and death, blessing and curses. Now choose life so that you and your children may live." Proverbs 18:21a says. "The tongue has the power of life and death."

I began to get revelation that the shortfall I was seeing was not God's perfect will for me, and that He had paid the price for my total freedom. The choice was ours and we were to choose life and life abundantly (see John 10:10), or we could choose to limit God by our natural ability to provide. The final decision on whether God would supply our needs according to His glorious riches in Christ Jesus (see Philippians 4:19) rested with us, not God. He already had the victory. It was our job to use the words of the Scriptures and to speak those things that be not as though they were (see Romans 4:17).

We began to stop looking at our physical financial limitations and began calling in God's blessing and provision. Tammie and I had said, "Lord if you could feed Elijah by the ravens in 1 Kings 17, then you can do the same thing for us." Whatever it took, we were going to receive God's best for Hannah and for us. We were givers and tithers and God would supply.

Within days people started calling and saying they had clothes, toys, supplies for our baby, and would we like them? We even came home one day and there were two bags full of baby things at our front door. Things started arriving in such abundance that there was not room enough to contain them (see Malachi 3:10). Hannah's room, our lounge and office began to spill over with all the things that began to arrive and before long we had to store stuff in our loft to make space downstairs.

At the time of this writing, Hannah is 3.5 years old and the clothes, toys and baby things continue to arrive. Other than food, nappies and a car seat, we have not had to buy anything for Hannah since she was born. God is so faithful and He is so good.

There have been so many other times when God has broken through with supernatural provision but I'll leave that for another book.

I pray that these testimonies encourage you to press deeper into God, find out what He has promised you in His word, lay hold of it and take it for your own lives. If God did it in Scripture, He can do it again; He does not change. If God did it for us He can do it for you.

9

Our Words are Powerful

The purpose of this chapter and chapter 10 is to help show us how to use the word of God as a practical tool in everyday life. The aim is to help unlock the scriptures and show us how to walk more in the victory that Jesus won on the cross.

Remember though, these are tools and not a formula. It's about a relationship with God, the Holy Spirit and His word. It's being obedient to what he says to you personally that brings about the final victory. What he said to me may not be what He is saying to you. I urge you to seek Him and His word and discover what He is saying to you in your situation. Also bear in mind that walking by faith in God's word is a process and results are not always instant. However the more we walk in His word and obey it, over time, the more consistently we begin to see more victory in our lives. Trouble will come and life doesn't always go the way we planned. Sometimes the results we see are not the results we hoped for. But I believe that God is the same yesterday, today and forever (see Hebrews 13:8). Ultimately whichever way a situation turns out God is somehow able to work it for our good (see Romans 8:28).

Chapter 9 and 10 are not meant to be a quick read. I encourage you to get your Bible out, study the scriptures, highlight them, meditate on them, pray over them and ask God to show you the truth of His word and how it practically applies to your situation. Take a few days or weeks to go over the scriptures in these chapters. Our lives are transformed when our minds are renewed (see Romans 12:2).

Re-teaching ourselves to think takes time and isn't always instant. We live in a world of instants but the 'suddenly' of God sometimes takes years to come to pass. We are to keep meditating on the Bible until what we see on the inside becomes more real than what we see on the outside. Then what's on the inside of us will frame up with what we see on the outside, and not the other way around. God's Kingdom is upside down. Seeing is not always believing. In God's Kingdom, what we believe is eventually what we see.

I believe the key to living in victory in everyday life and in every situation is not learning the Bible, or even just quoting the Bible. It's letting God's word come alive in us. It's letting God's word become our very source of life and feeding off it every day (see Matthew 4:4). Let the word of God become our source of information, not just what is going on in the world around us. The Bible says that as a man thinks in his heart so is he (see Proverbs 23:7). What we think on all the time is what we become. What we allow into our lives in abundance is what comes out of our lives in abundance (see Matthew 12:34). God's word is alive (see Hebrews 4:12); feed from it and let it give you life and life in abundance (see John 10:10).

Now some of you might disagree slightly with the next bit that I'm going to speak about. That's okay, we are all walking in the light that we have. This is what God has shown me. I most certainly don't understand everything about God and we are all trying to walk in the revelation we have. These are the things God is beginning to give me more understanding of.

Firstly, I am going to look at what the Bible really is. Some people see the Bible as just a book. The Bible is not just a book. It's the very essence of God Himself. The Bible is the very words of God on a page and the Holy Spirit brings it to life. We need to understand that God the Father, Jesus, and the Holy Spirit are one. Just thinking about that can flat-line our brains, but it's important to understand that although they are separate, they are all God and are one.

The Bible says that all scripture is God-breathed (see 2 Timothy 3:16). Therefore, all scripture came about by the breath of God. Everything in the Bible is from God the Father, the Son and the Holy Spirit. The Bible was created by the Holy Spirit breathing through man. So, the very essence of the Bible is actually from God himself. The Bible is full of the words of Jesus, the words of the Father and the words of the Holy Spirit.

Now let's look at some scripture that speaks of this:

John 1:1-4 NIV
1 In the beginning was the Word, and the Word was with God, and the Word was God. 2 He was with God in the beginning. 3 Through him all things were made; without him nothing was made that has been made. 4 In him was life, and that life was the light of all mankind.

Revelation 19:13-15a NIV
13 He is dressed in a robe dipped in blood, and his name is the Word of God. 14 The armies of heaven were following him, riding on white horses and dressed in fine linen, white and clean. 15 Coming out of his mouth is a sharp sword with which to strike down the nations.

Hebrews 4:12 NIV
12 For the word of God is alive and active. Sharper than any double-edged sword, it penetrates even to dividing soul and spirit, joints and marrow; it judges the thoughts and attitudes of the heart.

The Bible or the word of God is the very nature of God. The very words spoken in the Bible are from God and are still alive. As we read and meditate (constantly think on or ponder on) on the Bible, the Holy Spirit brings the word of God to Life. As we see in Revelation 19:13, Jesus is the word of God.

The weapon Jesus used was in his mouth. His sword that defeats every enemy is the sword in His mouth and it's His word that comes out of His mouth that brings life and life abundantly (see John 10:10). Just like Jesus, our words carry great power.

We need to get revelation of this truth as it's very important. What we meditate on (constantly think on or ponder on) gets into our hearts. Once it's in our hearts, our mouths will speak it out (see Luke 6:45). What is in our hearts is what we believe and what we believe in our hearts is what we have faith for and it's that thing that we speak that will come to pass in our lives. What ultimately comes out of our mouths on a consistent basis is the fruit we will see in our lives (see Proverbs 18:20-21).

A good example of the power we carry in our mouths can be seen in John the Baptist's father, Zechariah (story found in Luke 1). Zechariah was a priest of the Lord. One day an angel appears to him and tells him that he and his wife Elizabeth are going to have a child. His name is to be John. The angel Gabriel then tells Zachariah that John will be filled with the Holy Spirit and will turn many of the people of Israel back to God. Zachariah does not believe the angel Gabriel and as a result the angel silences Zachariah's tongue until the day that God's word would be fulfilled. Zachariah was not able to speak from that day forward until the birth of John the Baptist.

Now this might sound like a strange story, but I believe this is the point. According to Deuteronomy 30:19, and Proverbs 18:20-22, we have the ability to choose death or life for us and our children and death and life are in the power of our tongue. I believe Zachariah had the ability in his mouth to stop the plan of God by speaking doubt and unbelief. As a result the angel closed his mouth so he could not speak against the promise of God. Once the promise had been fulfilled and John was born, Zachariah was again able to speak.

Now I don't believe God shuts every person's mouth who speaks against His promises. But I do believe that this scripture is a practical example of just how much power we carry in our words and why it is so important to speak what God is saying and come into agreement with what heaven is doing in every situation. I believe God was making a point and was showing us that the only person who had the ability to stop God's plan was the person who God revealed the plan to. Zachariah had the ability to stop the plan with his words and so God closed his mouth until His plan came to pass. Are we speaking what God is saying or are we coming against the promises of God with our mouths?

Let's dig a little deeper in scripture. Let's have a look at why what we meditate on and why what we speak is so vitally important.

Right in the beginning of the Bible in Genesis 1 (go and read the whole chapter), we see the Spirit of God hovering over the Earth. God spoke and it was. From nothing seen in the natural world, He, through His word, created what is now seen in the natural. So, God called out of the invisible and made it visible. That's all very well, you might think, but what does that have to do with us?

Well, I'll tell you. I believe it has a lot to do with us.

In Genesis 1:26 we are told that we are made in the image of God and in Genesis 2:7 we are shown that God breathed His breath into our lives. We are made in the very likeness of God and we have access to the same creative power God has. This creative power is demonstrated in the words that come out of our mouths. What we store up in our hearts comes out of our mouths and calls those things which be not as though they were (see Romans 4:17).

I believe the problem with a lot of us is we are using this sword (our words) coming out of our mouths in the wrong direction. We are filling our lives with the world's systems, with the lies of the devil, with fear, with lust, with destruction, and then when we hit a crisis, we want God to intervene and change our situation. But Matthew 12:37 tells us that by our words are we justified and by words are we condemned. So what we say really matters. Just like Proverbs 6:2 explains, sometimes our lives can become trapped by the words we have spoken.

Unfortunately the harvest we may be living in today may be from the seed/words that we sowed in days gone past (see Galatians 6:7). Please don't misunderstand me. I'm not saying that every problem in our lives is from what we speak as Jesus told us that in this world we would have trouble (see John 16:33). Problems will come, but the way we navigate through them and overcome them absolutely has everything to do with what we are full of and what we declare out of our mouths in faith or fear.

Faith or fear both work. The Bible says that faith is the assurance of things hoped for and the conviction of things not seen (see Hebrews 11:1) and faith comes by hearing (see Romans

10:17). What we are constantly hearing, believing and then constantly speaking is what we have faith for and that makes our way prosperous either for good or bad (see Joshua 1: 8). Job also said, "What I feared has come upon me" (see Job 3:25).

So what we think about all the time is what we are meditating on and that is what we have faith for when it comes out of our mouths. This may sound harsh but that's the key right there; it's what's in our heart in abundance that will come out of our mouth in faith. It's these words that carry great power because words mixed with faith produce results.

Let's look at some scripture in order to understand more.

Ephesians 6:16-17 NIV
16 In addition to all this, take up the shield of faith, with which you can extinguish all the flaming arrows of the evil one. 17 Take the helmet of salvation and the sword of the Spirit, which is the word of God.

So, in every circumstance we need to take up the shield of faith and, according to Romans 10:17, faith comes by hearing and hearing by the word of God. The very thing that protects us from harm in every circumstance in life is the word of God and the more we hear the word and get it in us, the more we are protected by the shield.

Now don't get me wrong. The shield of faith doesn't stop the arrows coming, but it does stop them having a lasting effect on us. Having more faith doesn't always cause every situation to go exactly the way we want it, but ultimately it protects us completely no matter which way the situation goes, good or bad. If we look at verse 17 it says that the sword of the Spirit is the word of God. When the word of God comes out of our mouths in faith it is a weapon and it's that weapon that defeats satan. In order to get the sword working for us and for God, we need to understand the power that the words that come out of our mouths have.

Let's look at some scriptures that speak of the power of our words and what the effect of what comes of our mouths is. I'm going to quote the scriptures first and then will comment on them.

Deuteronomy 30:19 NIV
19 This day I call the heavens and the earth as witnesses against you that I have set before you life and death, blessings and curses. Now

choose life, so that you and your children may live

Proverbs 18:20-21 NIV
20 From the fruit of their mouth a person's stomach is filled; with the harvest of their lips they are satisfied. 21 The tongue has the power of life and death, and those who love it will eat its fruit.

Matthew 12:33-37 NIV
33 "Make a tree good and its fruit will be good, or make a tree bad and its fruit will be bad, for a tree is recognized by its fruit. 34 You brood of vipers, how can you who are evil say anything good? For the mouth speaks what the heart is full of. 35 A good man brings good things out of the good stored up in him, and an evil man brings evil things out of the evil stored up in him. 36 But I tell you that everyone will have to give account on the Day of Judgment for every empty word they have spoken. 37 For by your words you will be acquitted, and by your words you will be condemned."

James 3:4-6 NIV
4 Or take ships as an example. Although they are so large and are driven by strong winds, they are steered by a very small rudder wherever the pilot wants to go. 5 Likewise, the

tongue is a small part of the body, but it makes great boasts. Consider what a great forest is set on fire by a small spark. 6 The tongue also is a fire, a world of evil among the parts of the body. It corrupts the whole body, sets the whole course of one's life on fire, and is itself set on fire by hell.

John 15:7 NIV
7 If you remain in me and my words remain in you, ask whatever you wish, and it will be done for you.

Our words carry great power; in fact they carry life and death in them. We have the power through what we believe and carry in our hearts to speak life or death into every situation. We have the power in our tongues and in our words. When we speak, our words steer our life in the direction we are speaking.

The key is we need to decide what we believe and with whom we are going to partner. We will generally partner with whom, or what, we know the most. If we are full of God and His word, we will partner with Him. If we are full of the things of the world and the lies of the devil, we will generally partner with him. So I urge you to make a decision not to follow the devil but rather to partner with, and follow God.

If we have been heading in the wrong direction, there is no need to fear. Don't let the devil lie to you and tell you that you are too far gone. Just repent and ask God to put you on His path again. Repent of the words you have spoken against God and His word and begin speaking God's plans and His word over your life. The blood of Jesus is more than enough for everyone and God casts our sins as far as the east is from the west (see Psalm 103:12). God's plans are to prosper us and not to harm us; they are plans for a hope and a future (see Jeremiah 29:11).

In every season and every situation I encourage you to choose life and choose God's word and take God's word as the final authority over your life.

I've discovered that life doesn't always go the way we think it should as our thoughts are not always God's thoughts (see Isaiah 55:8). I don't understand why bad things happen sometimes. But I do know that as we continue to say what God says about us, our words have the ability to turn the direction we are going in. I believe God is a good God and when all is said and done He will work all things for our good if we continue to love Him (see Romans 8:28).

10

Tools to Help Renew Our Minds

As in Chapter 9, don't just read over this but meditate on it. Get your Bible out, search the truths and make it your reality too.

I believe having a sound mind is part of our inheritance as believers. Jesus has paid the price so that we can walk free and in victory in every area of our lives, including having a sound mind that is free from any spiritual demonic activity.

The Bible speaks a lot about having a sound mind and walking free of mental worries. Now

I'm not a doctor or counsellor, and I believe in both and getting the right help when you need it. I also know that not all mental struggles are spiritual, the brain and the mind are very complex and there is wisdom in pursuing all avenues when you are walking through struggles, and that includes seeking professional help when needed.

But as described earlier in this book, I have had my fair share of mental attacks and spiritual struggles. I have had to learn how to stand firm against Satan's attack in my mind. These are some of the scriptures and Biblical tools God has used to show me that freedom belongs to me. They are tools and truths I have, and continue to stand on to remain free from fear, worry and anxiety. I encourage you to take these scriptures, meditate on them, and ask God for your own revelation.

The Bible says that by being anxious we will not be able to add even an hour to our lives (see Matthew 6:27). In other words, worrying about things does us no good and it doesn't change anything anyway. Somehow we think that we are being responsible by worrying about an issue or a problem. Biblically though, by worrying about issues and problems we are actually being irresponsible, because God is our Father and He takes care of us. God takes all of our cares and he gives us a sober mind. He is our caretaker, not us (see 1 Peter 5:7-8). Having a sober mind means to have a mind that is not under the influence of anything other than God. Worry and fear are not from God; God has not given us a spirit of fear but He has given us a sound mind, power and love (see 2 Timothy 1:7). So, according to the Bible, we are to resist fear and choose to think on God and whatever things are good (see Philippians 4:8).

But the choice is ours. Jesus paid the price for our total victory and in Him we can choose to have a sound mind.

Let's look at some other scriptures:

Deuteronomy 30:19 NIV
19 This day I call the heavens and the earth as witnesses against you that I have set before you life and death, blessings and curses. Now choose life, so that you and your children may live

Isaiah 53:4 NIV
4 Surely he took up our pain and bore our suffering, yet we considered him punished by God, stricken by him, and afflicted.

Psalm 34:18 NIV
18 The Lord is close to the broken-hearted and saves those who are crushed in spirit.

So we can see that God has laid life and death before us, but we need to choose what we believe. In Isaiah 53:4 the word "pain" in Hebrew can also mean physical and mental pain. So, Jesus not only died for our physical pain but also for our mental pain.

The Hebrew meaning of the word hearted in Psalm 34:18 can also mean "mind." So God is close to us when we feel like we have a broken mind and he can save us from a spirit that feels crushed and defeated.

I don't believe everything I think, as not all my thoughts are from me. Some are from God, some are from me and some are from the devil.

Quite simply, the way I see it, is there are only four sources of spiritual thoughts or voices. There are our thoughts or voice, God's thoughts or voice, the devil's thoughts or voice and an angel's voice. Each time a thought or voice comes into my mind, I consciously think about from where this thought originates.

For example, if I'm on a train and suddenly I have a thought that there may be a terrorist attack on this train and that I might die. If I keep on thinking down that line, before I know it I could be in tears, screaming in terror and having a full-blown panic attack.

One of the keys I've learned is this. When the thought first enters my mind, I ask myself where this thought is coming from. Well, firstly, this thought is probably not from me; I like to live and so I am not going to plan my own demise.

Could this thought be from God? Well, according to Jeremiah 29:11, God knows the plans He has for me, plans to prosper me and not to harm me. Well, this thought is about my harm, so therefore the thought is not from God. That only leaves one other source; this thought must be from the demonic realm.

Understanding where the thought is from is one thing, but breaking free from its grip is another. In order to understand how to break free, I'm going to look at one of the ways I've learned how the spirit of fear works. Most thoughts that are from the devil will always have an element of fear attached to them. Fear is a funny thing. For me, fear very seldom starts off as full-blown terror or panic.

I believe fear knocks at the door of our minds and we open the door, not realising what we are doing. The more we let it in, the more it moves in and the quicker the path from a thought to paralysing fear develops. What once took hours of dreadful thoughts to arrive at a disaster in our heads, can now take seconds.

Well, what happened? How did this thought go from me thinking there might be a terrorist attack to me having a panic attack, in just a few minutes in my head?

I would like to suggest this is what happened in the spiritual realm. The Bible says, knock and the door will be opened (see Matthew 7:7). Imagine our minds as a gate into a house. We have the keys to unlock the gate. We can let in those thoughts we want and keep the gate locked to keep the thoughts out we don't want. I believe fear knocks at the gate of our minds. Instead of telling it to leave and showing it that the gate is locked. We allow the fear to convince us that the lock is actually open. We begin to question whether the gate is locked and don't enforce our authority by showing the fear that it has no right to enter our mind. We begin to doubt and before we know it, fear has come through the gate and is now sitting in the living room of our mind so to speak.

Just like the scripture says: knock and the door will be opened. Fear knocked and we unknowingly opened the door to it. This fear then begins to take over our minds. It's a bit like someone forcing themselves into our house. We could have stopped them but they threatened us, so we let them enter. They then sit down, watch our TV, change the channels and order us around to cook some food for some of their friends that are also coming around for a visit later. Suddenly, we became the slave to an unwanted guest, when we could have just kept the gate closed and not allowed them to enter, in the first place.

The point is, the devil is always roaming around like a lion, looking for someone to devour (see 1 Peter 5:8-9). Instead of letting him devour us, we are to resist him and he will flee from us (see James 4:7). Jesus paid the price for our freedom and he has given us the keys to the kingdom (see Matthew 16:19). Our minds belong to the Kingdom of God. If we've given our lives to Jesus and His Spirit is in us then He is the king of our lives. The gates of our mind are locked to the devil and open to God.

We need to look at it like this. In Heaven there is no fear and so when Heaven meets Earth in our life, there should be no fear. God's plan for our lives is Earth as it is in Heaven (see Matthew 6:10). So, actually fear has no right to be in our minds.

When we see that fear at the gate of our mind, we might feel fear, because fear is a spirit (see 2 Timothy 1:7) and therefore we can sense its presence in the spiritual realm. Just because we can sense it, does not mean it has any authority over us though. We have the keys to the Kingdom and our minds are part of God's Kingdom rule. Fear may knock at the gate but we're not letting it in. Fear does not have to be allowed in our minds. The only one allowed in is Jesus. He can have governance of our mind, not the devil. However, we are the ones who stand guard over our own minds and we have to enforce our authority as to what comes into our minds or not. I can't do that for you and you can't do that for me.

I believe fear is a master of illusion and it is from the devil. The Bible even calls the devil the father of lies (see John 8:44). I think this is probably more accurate of what is actually happening spiritually when fear tries to enter in. This is more like how the devil acts.

Imagine there is a snake who thinks that he owns the whole world. He has a big loud speaker around his neck telling everyone how scary he is and how sick he can make us if he bites us. This snake's big tactic is intimidation and he uses it to his full advantage. He always uses shadows to reflect a big image and we never really see who he is, just the projected shadow. Snakes can be pretty scary and a big one in front of your face, fangs out ready to bite you, is even worse. This snake uses these pictures in our minds to keep our attention and keep us in fear, constantly reminding us that if we get out of line, he will bite us.

But, the fact is, compared to who we are and how big God inside us is, this nasty, scary sounding thing is still at the end of the day just a little snake. That's why Psalm 2 tells us that the Lord sits enthroned and laughs at the devil's schemes.

The devil will always try casting a shadow of over us. Sometimes it's a shadow of doubt, a shadow of fear or a shadow of intimidation, but that's all it is: a shadow. It's time we get up and come out from that shadow and tell this snake to leave us alone. We belong to God and are supposed to be under His shadow and shelter. Under His shadow is peace and protection (see Psalm 91:1).

I believe it's all about perspective. If we get down on the floor and look at the snake eyeball to eyeball, it can look very frightening. We might even think we will die if it bites us. But if we get up, take a step or two back, suddenly this snake looks small. Imagine then getting in an aeroplane and flying at 30 000 feet, what was so intimidating on the floor can't even be seen anymore. We are called to soar high like eagles (see Isaiah 40:31), not be on the floor with the snakes. Eagles eat snakes, not the other way around. We need to look at our circumstances from God's perspective and realise who we are in Him. The Bible says that the God of peace will soon crush satan under our feet (Romans 16:20a). When we abide in God and He in us, we are lifted high, far above fear (see John 15:4, Psalm 91:11-14, Ephesians 1:21).

I will explain how I'm practically walking this out in the confession declarations part of this chapter.

We need to get to know the word of God and get it in us, so that when the lies of the enemy come, we can combat them with the knowledge of Jesus and the knowledge of the word.

2 Corinthians 10:3-6 NIV:
3 For though we live in the world, we do not wage war as the world does. 4 The weapons we fight with are not the weapons of the world.

On the contrary, they have divine power to demolish strongholds. 5 We demolish arguments and every pretension that sets itself up against the knowledge of God, and we take captive every thought to make it obedient to Christ. 6 And we will be ready to punish every act of disobedience, once your obedience is complete.

We are to take every thought captive and make it obedient to Christ. A lot of the mental struggles I have experienced are lies and arguments that the devil gets me to think. He wants me to think on thoughts of calamity, thoughts of destruction, thoughts of disaster, thoughts of death and a whole host of other thoughts.

Often I've tried to win the battle in my mind and said something like, "Thought I take you captive in Jesus' name." This may work initially but it might not work for long. 2 Corinthians 10 tells us to destroy arguments and everything else raised against us with the knowledge of God. The key here is the knowledge of God. The more I know God and His nature, the more I will walk free. The more I get to know God's word (the Bible), the more victory I experience.

Keeping the gates of our minds locked to the enemy's attack is to choose God and His thoughts and words. We are not to think on what the devil tells us to think about. I have found it very difficult to fight thoughts with thoughts though. We need to fight thoughts with words, and more specifically the word of God, as this brings life to every situation. The Bible says faith comes by hearing and hearing by the word of God (see Romans 10:17). When we hear the word of God, it brings faith to our situation. Did you notice that it didn't say faith comes by thinking? Faith comes by hearing. If we want faith to overcome evil thoughts, then we need to speak God's words and hear them with our own ears. God's words have the ability to change every situation in our lives, including our thoughts.

Here's a practical example of how I have done this.

Let's imagine that I'm struggling with thoughts of fear. Every time that thought comes, I say out loud, so that I can hear it. I say, "Thought you listen to me, I take you captive right now in Jesus' name. God's word said in Philippians 4:8 that I can choose what I think about. So right now I choose to think about God's love for me and His perfect love for me casts out all fear. So fear I refuse to receive you and I resist you and you will flee from me now in Jesus' name" (see 1 John 4:18, James 4:7).

I can consciously make a decision and change my line of thinking. I don't have to try and defend myself and create a case trying to prove my innocence against the thoughts of the devil. I open my mouth and start declaring the truth of who God is and who I am in Him.

Sometimes, however, the thoughts of the devil may be really intense and I can't even remember what the Bible says.

What then?

Well, then I still say, "Thought I take you captive," and I begin to thank God for anything that I can think of. I thank him for my hands, my feet, the fact that I'm breathing. I thank him for my wife and as I get going I begin to remember more and more of what I'm thankful for. Joy begins to fill my mind and fear and dread have gone. What am I doing? I am submitting myself to God, resisting the devil and he has fled from me (see James 4:7). I'm reminding myself that God loves me and that everything I'm thanking Him for is an expression of His love for me. Then His love casts out the fear (see1 John 4:18).

This takes practice, but I've seen it work for me. I've had to train my mind what to think. Philippians 4:8 tells us to think about whatever is pure, lovely and praiseworthy. The devil wants us to think anxious thoughts. But God's word says we must think on Him; His thoughts bring peace even when we don't understand how things can work out. We don't need to understand how it's going to work out; God knows, and He will work it out in our favour (see Romans 8:28).

I have found great victory in this technique; getting hope to rise up in my spirit and to stir up the gift of faith that God has given me. I believe you too have the potential to change the way you think but you need to speak it into being. The authority is in our mouth, not our heads.

The devil is always looking to engage us in an argument with him and then we spend all day trying to defend ourselves, even with Scripture. This strategy gets us spending all of our time meditating on the lies of the devil wondering if God will actually deliver us. Let's not do that; just change the subject and change the thought and make our minds think on the good things of God. We don't need a lawyer or a defence team for the lies; Jesus already paid the price for our freedom and we win the case every time. The past is the past and thirty seconds ago is also the past. If you've done something wrong, repent and ask God for forgiveness and it's gone.

We press on towards the goal and prize that God has for us. We're no longer condemned; God has thrown our sins as far is the East is from the West. We're free and the old has gone and the new has come in our life (see Philippians 3:12-14, Romans 8:1-2, Psalm 103:12, Galatians 5:1, 2 Corinthians 5:17).

So, when the devil lies to us, just laugh it off and say "HA, HA, devil, that's not my thought and I'm not thinking it anymore in Jesus' name."

We shouldn't worry if we feel intimidated by the idea of laughing at the thought. Just do it, even if you have to do it by faith. I've been intimidated many times, but the more I've laughed and praised God the more strength has come and the easier it has got. The joy of the Lord is becoming my strength (see Nehemiah 8:10).

Jesus has already delivered us; He has made a public spectacle of the devil (see Colossians 2:15). The devil has been defeated. The high court of Heaven has already sat and Jesus won the victory. We are hidden in Him and the victory He won belongs to us too. We are to transform our lives by the renewing of our minds (see Romans 12:2).

We are to get the word of God in our mouths in abundance and speak to that mountain and tell it to cast itself into the sea (see Mark 11:23). We are to speak to those thoughts, those voices and tell them about our great God and what He has done, what He has accomplished and who we are in Him. We are to continue to meditate on the words of God day and night until we make our way prosperous (see Joshua 1:8).

Here is a practical confession you can declare on a regular basis out of your mouth. I've made it a habit for myself and I've found great victory in it, so I included it for you to make your own too. It's the truth of God's word and Jesus said, "Then you will know the truth and the truth will set you free" (John 8:32 NIV). Type this confession declaration out, stick this on your walls, in your car or carry it around with you. Keep the Bible in front of your eyes and keep it coming out of your mouth all the time. As you submit yourself to God and resist the devil, he will flee from you (James 4:7).

CONFESSION DECLARATION

God, your word says that the thoughts you think towards me are thoughts to prosper me and not to harm me. They are thoughts of good and plans for a future (see Jeremiah 29:11). God you have not given me a spirit of fear but of love, power and a sound mind (see 2 Timothy 1:7). God, your word says in Isaiah 55:10-11 (paraphrased) that your word does not return to you void, so I speak your words because they bring life and life in abundance (see John 10:10).

I refuse to fear because Jesus you love me and you said in John 16:27 that the Father loves me. Psalm 91:14 tells me that because I love you and you already love me, you will deliver me and honour me with long life and show me your salvation.

So, Jesus I thank you that your perfect love for me casts out all fear (see 1 John 4:18) and I command every thought of calamity and disaster or whatever else to leave now in the name of Jesus.

Psalm 91:10 says (paraphrased) that no disaster shall come near my tent. Psalm 34:4 NIV says, "I sought the Lord and he answered me; he delivered me from all of my fears." Verse 19 says, "The righteous person may have many troubles, but the Lord delivers him from them all."

I am the righteousness of God through faith in Christ Jesus (see Romans 3:22) and I speak the plans God has for me over my life. Proverbs 18:10 says (paraphrased) the name of the Lord is a strong tower and the righteous (that's me) run to it and they are safe.

Psalm 91 tells me that you will cover me and hide me and in you I'm safe and protected. The devil can't get to me because he has to come through you, because I'm in you. Colossians 3:3 tells me I'm hidden in Christ.

So, right now, I renew my mind (see Romans 12:2) and I use the name that is above every name (see Philippians 2:9-10). I speak to this thought, voice, sickness or mountain and I command it to leave me in Jesus' name (see Mark 11:23).

I make a decision to stand on the word of God and I refuse to be shaken and refuse to move (see Ephesians 6:10-17). I declare that the word of God is the final authority in my life and no matter how long it takes to achieve victory, I refuse to back down. God's word is true and His ways are right.

I come into agreement with His words (see Matthew 18:19) and choose God's plan for my life and I will call those things which be not as though they are in my life (see Romans 4:17). If healing be not, then I call down healing from heaven right here on Earth.

If peace be not, then I call peace down from Heaven. Matthew 18:18 says (paraphrased) if it's been loosed in Heaven I can loose it on Earth. If healing is available in Heaven, then I have it here on Earth; if blessing is available in Heaven, then I have it on Earth; if peace and a sound mind are available in Heaven then I have them on Earth.

In Matthew 6:10 Jesus prayed, "on earth as it is in heaven." So, if strife and turmoil in the mind, evil thoughts, wicked voices, lack in any form are not allowed in Heaven, then they are not allowed in my life here on Earth. And I refuse to quit because there is reward for me as I stand (see Galatians 6:9, Hebrews 10:23, 35 -39).

I receive these promises in my life in Jesus' name.

I encourage you to get to know God, get into His word and chase after the abundant life that He has for us.   I urge you to choose life and life abundantly. Choose to think on the things of God and not the things of the devil. I still use these tools often and continue to stand and walk in more victory.

You can download this Confession Declaration for free at
http://www.livinginvictoryministries.com/reso

urces/confession-declaration/

11

Conclusion

I trust and pray that through this book God has revealed Himself more to you. His goodness is not dependent on the circumstances or situations we find ourselves in.

Hearing my story might leave you filled with faith, or sceptical that these stories could even be real. Don't worry I too used to have difficulty understanding why I kept walking through so many trials. The constant battle seemed surreal and pointless. After all, I'm just a normal guy, why did difficulties keep seeking us out? I spent many moments irritated with God and frustrated with life.

Constantly comparing my life with friends who (from the outside at least) didn't seem to walk through the same level of hardship as us.

Only when the Lord began speaking to me about writing this book did my story begin to make more sense. My perspective started to change. What I used to think was "ALL ABOUT ME," suddenly became "ALL ABOUT GOD." God could use my story to bless and encourage other people who were still walking through the "test" of their testimony.

I have made a decision that God is good all the time, even when I don't understand His ways and things don't make sense.

Truthfully there have been some situations that have not gone the way we wanted, no matter how much we trusted God or spoke His word. People have died that we wanted God to heal, and some breakthroughs didn't come through in the time frame we expected. Somehow, God didn't move in the way we wanted Him to move.

I guess, in the midst of great breakthrough, trusting God for victory, there is a line of tension between the "now and the not yet" in our lives. What I mean is this, even with the greatest faith, best confessions and completely trusting God, there is still an element of the mystery of God that we don't yet entirely understand. Somehow, the Kingdom of God has fully come and yet at the same time is still coming in our lives. It is a mystery to me and one of the greatest questions I think we will face in our Christian walk. How is it that we can we see such great victory trusting God and yet in the midst of that, at times experience what seems like great defeat?

Truthfully, I don't have all the answers. At times, I have grieved, and been disappointed with life and questioned God's goodness. In those seasons I have needed to remind myself that I have seen the goodness of God in the past and have tried to keep this truth in front of my eyes and remind myself that God will get me through this. Trust me, I know that is so easy to say and have preached to you, but in reality, it can be so difficult to live out in a season of great struggle. Take heart and take courage and lift up your eyes, God is close to the broken hearted, and He saves those who are crushed in spirit (See Psalm 34:18).

In the light of eternity, I'm sure these things will make perfect sense. Until then though, I choose to believe that God is good and trust Him. I have faith that when all is said and done, somehow God will work even these hard situations for our good. I pray you will do the same.

Don't judge God's goodness from what you may be seeing in the present moment; give Him some time, and you will see that He was there all the time. He never left you; He has never forsaken you. Tough seasons are exactly that, A SEASON, and seasons always change. Though sorrow may last for a night, joy comes in the morning. I encourage you to look up and look to God as He is good and He is the author and perfecter of our faith.

God loves you and wants to invite you into a deeper relationship with Him. The closer you get to Him the more breakthroughs you will see. Intimacy is the key, not just information about God or even other people's testimonies. The more you fall in love with Jesus the more you will be like Him and want to do what He says - even when it doesn't make sense. God is not a formula, He is alive and wants a deeper relationship with you, and He loves you. He wants to whisper the secrets of victory to you. I pray God would give you eyes to see and ears to hear what He is doing and saying to you personally.

God can use my testimony and teaching to inspire and encourage you but what He says to you, may be different than what He said to me. Now some of you might find that discouraging but I find it really encouraging. This tells me that God loves us each intimately and individually. He has a personal word of victory and breakthrough for each one of us in our circumstance and situation. I encourage you to get into God's word, make it your life. It's not just a book, but rather it's the very essence of God Himself. God is able to heal, prosper, protect, deliver and redeem you from any of life's situations. Fight the good fight of faith because He who has promised is faithful. God will do what He said in His word. Find out what He said, make it yours and take your victory by faith. Give everything to Jesus; He is trustworthy, and He wants you whole. He died and rose again for your victory.

12

Make Jesus the Lord of Your Life

If you haven't made Jesus the Lord of your life and you don't know Him as Saviour, then don't go another day without giving your life to Him. It's the best decision you will ever make.

Simply pray these words. Jesus I want to give my life to you. I ask you to forgive me of all my sins. I recognise you as the King of Kings and the Lord of Lords. I want you to be my King. I renounce the devil and everything he stands for. From this day, my life belongs to Jesus and Lord, I ask that you would take my life and do something with it.

It tells us in Romans 10:9 that if you declare with your mouth, "Jesus is Lord," and believe in your heart that God raised him from the dead, you will be saved.

So, today I have declared with my mouth and believe in my heart that Jesus is Lord and I believe I am saved.

This is the best decision you have ever made. Now go and tell a friend, find a church that preaches the Bible and get into God's word.

Jesus loves you and in Him you can do anything.

Get This Book into the Hands of People Who Need it.

If you enjoyed this book then please let us know about it. If you brought it on Amazon please leave us a positive review. If you did not like it rather keep it to yourself.

Most of the people who will benefit from this book may never find it. Please tell as many people as you can about this book, share the links on your Facebook, talk about it, Tweet about it and get it into the hands of those who need to see God's goodness through any season of life. Be a blessing to those people you feel would benefit from this book and get them a copy.

Connect with Byron on Facebook at https://www.facebook.com/livinginvictoryChristianencouragement/

We will trust God with you to impact as many lives as possible with this book.

Many thanks,
Byron and Tammie

TESTIMONIES *of a* GOOD GOD

About the Author

Byron van der Merwe is married to Tammie. They have a daughter, Hannah and recently welcomed baby Joshua into the family. They live in Hampton, just outside of London, England. Both Byron and Tammie are passionate about local church and are very involved in a church called Kingsgate Church in Kingston upon Thames, London England.

Byron is a passionate speaker. If you would like him to come and share at your event please go to http://www.livinginvictoryministries.com/christian-speaker/ for more details.

Download Your Exclusive Free Video Teaching Today

WATCH YOUR FREE VIDEO NOW

Receive the latest Blog-posts and updates directly to your inbox. You can unsubscribe at any time.

Don't worry we hate spam too. You details are never shared.